CYBERSECURITY FOR EVERYONE

Securing your home
or small business network

Terence L. Sadler

SIGNALMAN PUBLISHING

Cybersecurity for Everyone
Securing your home or small business network
by Terence L. Sadler

Signalman Publishing
www.signalmanpublishing.com
email: info@signalmanpublishing.com
Kissimmee, Florida

ISBN: 978-1-940145-36-5 (paperback)
978-1-940145-37-2 (ebook)

LCCN: 2014958499

LINKS TO THIRD PARTY SITES

Cybersecurity for Everyone contains links to websites as references to related material. The web sites are not under the control of the author, and the author is not responsible for the contents of any website, including without limitation any link contained in a referenced web, or any changes or updates to a referenced website. The author is not responsible for webcasting or any other form of transmission received from any referenced web site. The author is providing these links to you only as a convenience, and the inclusion of any link does not imply endorsement by the author of the site or any association with its operators.

LIABILITY DISCLAIMER

The information, software, products, and services described herein may include inaccuracies or typographical errors. Changes are periodically added to the information herein. The author and/or its publisher may make improvements and/or changes in the cotent at any time. Advice received via the "cybersecurty for everyone" book or e-book should not be relied upon for personal, medical, legal or financial decisions, and you should consult an appropriate professional for specific advice tailored to your situation.

The author and/or its publisher make no representations about the suitability, reliability, availability, timeliness, and accuracy of the information, software, products, services and related graphics contained in the "cybersecurity for everyone" for any purpose. To the maximum extent permitted by applicable law, all such information, software, products, services and related graphics are provided "as is" without warranty or condition of any kind. The author and/or its publisher hereby disclaim all warranties and conditions with regard to this information, software, products, services and related graphics, including all implied warranties or conditions of merchantability, fitness for a particular purpose, title and non-infringement.

SIGNALMAN PUBLISHING

ACKNOWLEDGEMENTS AND DEDICATION

To my wife and children who supported me throughout the writing of this book. They deserve special thanks because I could not have been successful if they had not allowed me the time I needed for what seemed like a very long journey. To my Dad who did not live to see me complete this book yet gave me encouragement all along the way while he could; thank you and I miss you daily. To my mom who continues to be an inspiration and encouragement; can you believe it?

Lastly, I want to thank everyone who has read my drafts, provided suggestions and encouraged me all along the way.

TABLE OF CONTENTS

Chapter One

Home User Computer Security Overview

Why Another Book on Computer Security?

I started using the Internet around 1993 without the benefit of a web browser. At that time, the Internet was a pretty safe place to visit. As with many things, when there is a social community of users from different backgrounds you'll find a wide array of behaviors ranging from good to very bad and downright perverted. The passing of time and new technologies has resulted in massive changes to our experience, and the Internet has become a global community. As with all communities, there are some sub-cultures who feed like piranha on others.

There are a lot of online resources available to help anyone interested in being safe on the Internet, but they are not comprehensive nor are they all in one place. My goal in writing this book is for anyone, regardless of technical background, to be able to look up a specific topic and implement the presented ideas to make their online experience safer. I also hope everyone will exercise the principle of reciprocity by passing on the knowledge they gain and help someone else reap the benefits of their experience.

The book is written to allow you to take it as a whole or pick and choose what works best for your situation and knowledge level. There are topics on specific operating systems, open source projects that are free for anyone to use, and best practices taken from my experience over 30 years working with technology, security, and risk management. I didn't learn everything at once and many of the concepts presented reflect my roots as a Cryptologist in the best Navy in the world and as a Security Specialist for the best Army in the world.

Common Sense Approach to Security

Using the computer shouldn't be so complicated it takes a degree in computer science to know what steps you can take to stay relatively safe. I say relatively safe because safe is an ideal or standard we like to believe exists. Unfortunately, the Internet is not as safe as we would like it to be even though you may never experience a negative consequence as a result of using the Internet.

When I was young and growing up in a small country community in Louisiana, almost no one locked their doors; even when going into town for the day. No one worried about their home being vandalized or belongings being stolen. Today in this same community, many people would not dream of leaving their doors unlocked when they go into town.

The only thing that has really changed is our culture and the paradigm through which we relate to our environment. In reality, we were no safer when I was growing up than we would be today if the person who wanted to vandalize our home or steal from us had been determined to do us harm. Our goal with computer security is to put up a few road blocks, lock a few doors, set a few alarms, and hope we don't have a determined attacker purposely going after us. Through it all we may even find a few good tools you can use to enhance your security even if we are not able to shoot back. Let me illustrate with an analogy from the early days of the AIDS pandemic. If you wanted to keep yourself safe from contracting AIDS you practiced abstinence or monogamy and hoped your partner was also monogamous. The same is true about using your computer.

If you want to keep yourself safe from the dangers of the Internet, you need to cut the umbilical cord and stay off the Internet. You should never install software or programs from untrusted sources and should consider storing your computer where no one else can access it without your permission. That's the only way to keep your computer safe from today's threats which use the Internet as their primary vector to launch attacks against unsuspecting victims.

If you want to use the Internet, then you must accept a certain level of risk and understand there may be consequences. Just like the analogy of AIDS, you might choose to use a condom, but while it will only provide a certain degree of protection which is not guaranteed, there may be consequences if the condom fails. Your computer use habits will impact how safe your computing experience will be.

We are going to look at habits and make an assessment of how risky each can be. If the habits we discuss present a good picture of your computer use habits, then you'll have a better idea of your level of risk and what you can do to change your habits.

In just about every city around the world, there are neighborhoods or locales where it's not real safe to venture out alone. The same can be said about the Internet. There are many websites purposely set up to trick users into believing they are legitimate or are in fact legitimate websites that have been compromised by attackers who will take advantage of any system vulnerabilities and weak security on your PC.

How can you tell the difference between a legitimate website and a fake website? It may not be that simple. Cyber criminals go to great lengths to make their websites seem legitimate. How can you tell if a website you are visiting has been compromised and is trying to circumvent your security settings? We'll try and answer these and other questions in the following chapters.

Sources for Software

When you have access to the Internet, you have access to a lot of software to be more productive with your computer. Some of the best software available today is free, but you need to be cautious when getting free software. I really recommend you check out software that uses one of the Open Source Initiative or Free Software Federation licenses as an option and stay away from software that does not allow its source code to be examined by others.[1][2]

There are also a lot of software programs peddled on the Internet that do nothing or almost nothing. These may be designed to do things with or to your computer you don't want happening such as keeping track of everything you type (key loggers), installing root kits, delivering malware, joining your computer to a botnet, or allowing a remote attacker to take control of your computer for any number of reasons.

How do you know good software from bad? Well, it can be challenging, but the best way to ensure you are getting good software is to read reviews, see how it is distributed and updated, see if there is a large community of users who help support the software through forums, etc. Stay away from "warez" websites that allow you to download cracked copies of pirated software.[3]

Yes, commercial software is expensive. Yes, it's tempting to download copies of commercial software when it's so easy to do. We can even talk ourselves into "trying" the software first before we spend money on it. Downloading pirated software is illegal and could land you in jail. Cyber criminals also like to distribute various types of malware by hiding it in pirated software or in Trojans using a dropper program. When you install pirated software or a Trojan that includes malware, it is installed without your knowledge using a dropper program.[4] This is very risky because the program is installed with privileged access since most operating systems require you to use administrator privileges to install software. Once you've authorized the installation you'll wind up with any number of different types of malware you will likely have a hard time getting rid of.

A dropper program installs malware without your knowledge on your computer when you are installing another program.[5] Hackers and cyber criminals are known to use pirated software to spread their malware because millions of unsuspecting people download pirated software, making it an excellent way to get inside your computer.[6]

Many Open Source software developers provide an MD5 Cryptographic Hash for their software. When you download Open Source software that is provided for free, you can check the download against the MD5 Cryptographic Hash provided by the developer. If the hash is identical, then you can be confident the program has not been altered by hackers or cyber criminals and should be safe.[7] As an example, Apache's OpenOffice website provides instructions on how you can verify the integrity of your OpenOffice download.[8]

Where Do We Begin?

There are a number of places we can begin to improve our security. Like I mentioned earlier, this book was written in a way to allow you to take it as a whole or pick and choose what works best for your situation. Since almost everyone who uses the Internet today is doing so using a broadband connection of some sort (cable modem, Digital Subscriber Line, satellite, WiMAX gateways, etc.) along with an integrated router or a separate router (wireless or wired), we'll start with steps one can take to improve security through the equipment you use to connect to the Internet.

We'll look at some of the basic configurations one can make in the router such as using network address translation (NAT), black listing or white listing media access control (MAC) addresses, and/or Internet Protocol (IP) addresses, changing default passwords and user names, setting up wireless security, and using a free or for fee service to filter malware (viruses, Trojans, rootkits, adware, pornography, and any other type of user definable content) before it reaches your network.

If you are not comfortable using an outside service, you can achieve some of the same results by using software designed for the same purpose. Let's get started by looking at the features of a few typical consumer modems/routers one is likely to find in a home, small school, church, community center, or even in a small business environment.

References

[1] THE OPEN SOURCE INITIATIVE. HTTP://OPENSOURCE.ORG/

[2] FREE SOFTWARE FOUNDATION. HTTP://WWW.FSF.ORG/

[3] WIKIPEDIA CONTRIBUTORS, "WAREZ," WIKIPEDIA, THE FREE ENCYCLOPEDIA, HTTP://EN.WIKIPEDIA.ORG/W/INDEX.PHP?TITLE=WAREZ&OLDID=616958055

[4] "Microsoft Malware Protection Center - Glossary." 2014. Accessed September 12. http://www.microsoft.com/security/portal/mmpc/shared/glossary.aspx.

[5] Lau, Hon. 2012. "Trojan.Dropper Technical Details | Symantec." http://www.symantec.com/security_response/writeup.jsp?docid=2002-082718-3007-99&tabid=2.

[6] "HACKERS EXPLOIT 'WATCH DOGS' RELEASE TO SPREAD BITCOIN MALWARE." 2014. CIRCA NEWS. ACCESSED SEPTEMBER 12. HTTP://CIR.CA/NEWS/MALWARE-WRITERS-EMBRACE-BITCOIN.

[7] Perrin, Chad. 2007. "Use MD5 Hashes to Verify Software Downloads." TechRepublic. http://www.techrepublic.com/blog/it-security/use-md5-hashes-to-verify-software-downloads/.

[8] "Apache OpenOffice - How to Verify the Integrity of the Downloaded File?" n.d. http://www.openoffice.org/download/checksums.html.

CHAPTER TWO

MODEMS & ROUTERS

Your modem provides the connectivity you need to access the Internet, and the addition of a router allows you to share the Internet connection among a number of devices. A typical home network may have several computers (laptop, desktop, netbook), game consoles, Internet enabled televisions, or video streaming devices.

So, what exactly is a modem? It is a device used to modulate and demodulate an analog carrier signal to transmit your computer's digital information.

A router is usually a separate piece of equipment that allows your modem to share the Internet connection, although some home and small business modems include an integrated router. Our focus will be on the steps you can take to configure a basic home or small business router, regardless of the make or model.

Access Control

Your router will have a default user name and password. One of the first things you should always do is change the password. If your router gives you the option of changing the user name, you should change the user name to something less obvious then the default user name.

For example, many Linksys or D-Link routers use **admin** as the default user name and password.[1] In some cases there is only a user name without an assigned password. Some routers will have admin as the user name and password as the default password. You really should change the default user name and password. Each make and model will provide different options which can be configured to im-

15

prove your security. It's always a good idea to take a few minutes and find out how to modify these settings in order to improve your home or small business network's security.

You should create a network configuration document to help you later if you forget the user name and password. A template for your network configuration document is provided in appendix three and is also available online from the Compass North Group, LLC website (www.cybersecurityforeveryone.com). See the chapter on encryption to learn about password protection for your network configuration documentation.

After you have changed the user name and password, you may want to consider setting up a white-list (allow Internet access) for your network. By creating a white-list, you are basically creating an access control list (ACL) for the devices in your network that are allowed to use the Internet through your router. Or you can create a black-list (deny Internet access) for devices that are not allowed to access the Internet.

One of the benefits of creating a white-list is that no other devices can connect through your router unless they are added to your white-list. This may be called something different in the documentation for your router. On some Linksys routers you'll find this under the "Access Restrictions" menu and then selecting the "Internet Access".

Keep in mind, at this point we are only configuring access to the Internet for devices that are physically connected to the router using an Ethernet cable. We'll look at wireless security later, but for now we are only looking at devices connected using Ethernet cables.

When you configure your router for either a white-list or black-list, you can use one of two address types. You can either use the device's Media Access Control address which is more commonly called the MAC, or you can use the device's Internet Protocol (IP) address. In most home networks, you will likely be using the Dynamic Host Configuration Protocol (DHCP) with Network Address Translation which is more commonly called NAT, so I generally recommend using the device's MAC address.

Each device capable of being connected to a home or small business network will have a MAC address. Most devices will have this address on a label near the plug where you connect the Ethernet cable. If it is not listed on a label, you may need to check your device's documentation to find the MAC address.

Once you have recorded the MAC address for all of the devices on your network configuration document, you are ready to add them to your router's configuration and save the changes.

One of the other benefits of using an access control list is the ability on some routers to define the day of week and number of hours individual devices are allowed to use the Internet. This feature is an excellent option for parents who do not want their children using the Internet unsupervised or only want to allow them to use it during certain hours. This will also keep your child's friends from bringing a personal laptop or other device into your home and accessing your network without your knowledge.

Another option your router may have is to limit the maximum number of DHCP users on your network to the number of devices you have in your home. If there are no IP addresses available, no new devices can be added without first removing a device or increasing the number of maximum allowed devices. Keep in mind, when a device is turned off it will not be connected to the network and the IP address provided by the DHCP service will become available to other devices. This will allow anyone to connect to your network if you are not using a white list with MAC filtering enabled.

Wireless Options

Wireless access control and security can be confusing at first because there are different configuration options similar to Ethernet. Even within the wireless router environment, you'll find different standards making it difficult to choose the best standard for your environment. We're going to look at the different standards and try to demystify them a bit.

Wireless routers are developed by the manufacturers based upon the 802.11 standard defined by the Institute of Electrical and

Electronics Engineers (IEEE). You will find routers defined upon 802.11a, 802.11b, 802.11g, 802.11n and more recently 802.11ac. The oldest defined standard is 802.11 with 802.11ac being the most common in routers on the market in 2014.

Each new standard improved performance and security over the previous standard. Most manufacturers try to maintain backwards compatibility with older standards, which can make transitioning to the new standard economical for small businesses or others who may have a lot of the older technology in their environment. The typical home user may decide to upgrade their environment right away or keep what they have until prices come down.

There are some key things you might consider when deciding to upgrade. Will you need to replace your network interface cards/ adapters or are they compatible with the new router/standard? If they are compatible, should they be replaced to take advantage of the newer standard? What advantage is there to upgrading? Is it related to performance, security, or both?

If it's performance, will your environment even benefit from the upgrade? If it's security, will it make a difference for your environment?

It can be confusing, but taking the time to understand the differences might save you a lot trouble and/or money. Wikipedia has a great page that describes the primary differences between each 802.11 standard and will help you understand some of the basics.[2]

I highly recommend you do some basic research for your specific router. Read the user guide provided with your router and visit the manufacturer's support website to see if there have been any software changes that may affect security. Each manufacturer implements the standards a little differently. This can make configuring your router easier, more difficult, or just provide you more or less control over the configuration. For example, some routers do not give the user control over the password or pass phrase set to enable Wi-Fi Protected Access (WPA) encryption, while some routers allow the user to set their own password or pass phrase.

There really are a lot of options available if you purchase your own router. If you are provided a router or modem by your Internet service provider (ISP), then you may have fewer options but you can still implement extra security. I use a cable ISP who provides my modem, but I also have a wireless router that allows me to control many of the features discussed in this chapter. I chose the router within my budget that gave me the greatest flexibility and control.

Wireless Security

You have several options when configuring security on your wireless router. These include not enabling any security, enabling Wired Equivalent Protection (WEP), or WPA/WPA2. I would never recommend not setting some wireless security if you have wireless devices on your network, unless you live on a country road by yourself where no one can approach your home without your knowledge. Typical consumer wireless routers have a maximum range of approximately 300 feet in free space, but when you add doors, walls, trees, shrubbery and other typical obstacles you find in an urban environment your maximum effective range is usually a good bit less.

If your only option is WEP, then you have a very old router and should upgrade to a newer wireless router because WEP can be broken in less than a minute. An interesting blog written in July 2012 by Ajay Gupta, a security professional for Infosecurity Magazine, reported many users in London were still either using no security or were still using WEP.[3]

I suspect we would find similar results across America, in spite of the fact many users have better security available on their current routers, but do not implement security because they do not understand how to configure their routers or just don't believe they are at risk. No security or WEP are not good options unless you live in a sanctuary where no one can get close enough to break into your network or try and leech your Internet connection. I don't want anyone to get the wrong idea though; I believe you should always use the best security practices available to protect the sensitive information stored on your computer.

This leaves us with WPA, which is actually a very good encryption protocol. When configured properly it will keep anyone from breaking into your network using most wireless attack methods.

A common theme you'll find repeated again and again when it comes to security is options. Depending on your router, there may be multiple options with WPA as well. Your router may give you any of the following options, which can seem confusing at first glance but are in fact describing the same features using different terminology. These are WPA, WPA Personal, WPA Enterprise, WPA2, WPA2 Personal, WPA2 Enterprise, or WPA with Temporal Key Integrity Protocol (TKIP).

Several of these options may also be described as WPA using a pre-shared key (PSK). So to clear up any ambiguity: WPA, WPA Personal, and WPA-PSK refer to the first version of WPA. WPA2, WPA2 Personal, WPA2-PSK refer to an enhanced version of WPA. The main differences between the personal or enterprise versions of WPA/WPA2 are key generation and authentication.

If you have a router that was manufactured prior to 2006 then you probably only have WEP or WPA as an option. All Wi-Fi CERTIFIED™ devices manufactured since 2006 are required to be WPA2 capable.[4] To take advantage of the best security available for your home network, you should implement WPA2. When configured properly with a lengthy complex password, WPA2 should keep your network secure from most wireless attack methods and provides an excellent level of security for the wireless segment of your network. In March 2014 a research report was published that describes a method to easily break WPA2 which is alarming but until a replacement or a security fix is developed WPA2 security is still the most secure option.[5]

Some routers do not give you the option of creating your own password, but will create a complex *passphrase* that is 20 or more characters in length. You should either record this passphrase in a password protected file or refer to your router's configuration document each time you add a device to your wireless network.

It would not be a good security practice to write the passphrase down and leave it where others can find it. The main reason for having security is to only allow devices you specifically approve on your network. If you write the passphrase down and your children know where you have it stored, they will be able to give this information to their friends, who will then be able to access your network without your knowledge or approval. Never underestimate the technical skills of your children or their friends.

Most criminals also know people will usually write their passwords and passphrases down on a piece of paper and hide them under the keyboard or in an easily accessible location at the desk. Don't write your passwords on a sticky note and stick it behind your monitor either. If you use a program that helps you organize and protect your passwords or take the time to create a password protected file with a complex password, then your passwords and passphrases will be better protected.

Wi-Fi Protected Setup (WPS) Vulnerabilities

WPS was designed by the Wi-Fi Alliance to make setting up consumer and small office/home office (SOHO) routers easier, and implement WPA to improve Wi-Fi security. Many routers for home use and the SOHO environment made since 2007 come with WPS enabled right out of the box.

WPS does make setting up WPA easy for anyone, but it is vulnerable to a brute force attack that would allow the attacker to recover your WPA keys and the PIN used with WPS, regardless of how long or complicated your password. If you are a home user, this may not really seem important to you. You may wonder how many people are really that interested in hacking into your network. If you are a small business owner, then you may actually be at greater risk to attack from hackers.

The attack can be done rather simply using a program called Reaver that is freely available for download on the Internet. The really scary thing about Reaver is that it can generally recover the target's plain text WPA/WPA2 passphrase in 4-10 hours, depending on the wireless router being attacked. In many cases, it doesn't take that much time to determine the correct WPS pin and recover the passphrase.

Sean Gallagher, an IT editor at Ars Technica, researched the WPS vulnerability after a paper was released by Stefan Viehböck describing the mechanics of the attack in 2011. Sean's research confirmed Stefan's findings and made an excellent observation and recommendation: "The bottom line is that, while WPS was designed for simple security, there is no such thing as simple security. The only way to be absolutely sure that someone can't gain access to your wireless network with the WPS hack is to make sure you use a router that doesn't support the WPS protocol". [6], [7]

Sean makes a good point, but like all recommendations you always want to consider your options. This is one security vulnerability hackers can exploit with minimal difficulty and one for which there doesn't seem to be a fix for many existing users, regardless of router manufacturer. You can implement a wireless ACL as I'll explain in the next section to reduce—but not eliminate—this vulnerability.

Wireless ACLs

Now that you've added wireless security, we can develop an access control list using either a white-list to allow devices or a black-list to deny access to the wireless, just like you can for devices using an Ethernet connection.

Why should you go to the trouble of creating a white-list or black-list? It all boils down to protecting your sensitive data like user names, passwords for shopping accounts, social network accounts, banking, schools, or other miscellaneous websites. It also ensures you do everything you can to keep personally identifiable information from falling into the wrong hands. If you live in an apartment complex or have neighbors within a few feet of your house, your efforts to secure your network will also keep others from leeching off of your Internet connection.

Once you've lost sensitive data, been hacked, or had your identity stolen, you will have to do a lot more work to regain some control than if you take time now to learn basic steps that will help protect you. The best article I've ever read about the risks of your accounts being hacked was written by James Fallows after his wife's Gmail account was hacked and hijacked. The hacker sent email to all of his wife's contacts telling them she was stranded in Madrid. I've included a link to the article in the references for this chapter. [8]

DNS Services

What exactly is a Domain Name System (DNS) Service you ask? You can think of DNS as the Internet's phone book. When you type in a web address in your browser's address bar, your Internet service provider's DNS server will check to see if it knows where to find the website you've requested. It does this by checking the web address against its cache of IP addresses. If it doesn't know where the web address is, the request will be forwarded to the next DNS server higher up the chain of servers until it locates the address you've requested. The DNS service translates the address you entered to the actual IP address of the server where your requested address can be found.

In more technical terms, the DNS is a distributed hierarchical database that allows computers, services, and any other resources on the Internet to resolve a domain name you enter into a web browser to the domain's IP address and return the webpage or object (file, etc.) in your browser.

DNS is essential for navigating the Internet and most ISPs provide your DNS services with their default network configuration, which in most cases is DHCP. Hackers and cyber criminals understand how important DNS is for the Internet and they have developed ways to take advantage of its inherent weaknesses.

They use DNS to lure unsuspecting victims to websites where they offer counterfeit merchandise. They create counterfeit websites of legitimate websites in order to steal login credentials or capture credit card information. They also set up websites specifically to spread malware by taking advantage of unpatched security vulnerabilities in operating systems and other popular applications such as Adobe Reader, Java, productivity suites, and more.

One way of adding another layer of security to your home or

small business network is to use one of the free or commercial DNS service providers that have been designed to enhance the security, safety, speed, and reliability of the Internet. These services allow you to leverage enterprise level security most average computer users don't have access to and will help prevent you from accidentally accessing known and other potentially dangerous websites.

When you use a DNS service, you have extra protection because any requests to a known malware site are usually blocked by the service automatically. Each of the DNS service providers I'll discuss in the next few paragraphs maintain an up to date database of malware, porn, and other malicious websites. A few of the DNS service providers business models are focused on making money from paying corporate customers, which allows them to offer the same or similar features for individuals and schools at a significantly reduced rate, or in some cases for free.

Setting up any of the DNS Service providers reviewed in the following paragraphs is pretty simple. All that needs to be done is add the DNS Service provider's DNS Server IP addresses to either your router configuration or to your computers network configuration. Don't worry. If this still sounds like a foreign language, each of the DNS service providers have easy to follow instructions on their websites to help you make the change and really add a great layer of security. A few of the DNS Service providers actually have wizards you can use to make setting up their service so easy anyone can do it without understanding how it works.

OpenDNS

OpenDNS is my favorite DNS security service provider. They have a free option and a fee-based personal version known as OpenDNS Home VIP. The OpenDNS Home VIP version was only $19.95 per year as of Sept 2014 and in my opinion is the most reasonable of all the for-fee providers when you consider everything they offer. OpenDNS gives you a lot more features than any of the other providers and they offer the kind of security one would only expect to find within large businesses, academic institutions, and government agencies.[9]

According to the OpenDNS marketing gurus you'll have the following features:

- Faster Internet and fewer outages due to DNS problems.

- Parental controls that allow you to filter out 56 categories of specific types of websites (pornography, games, academic fraud, social media) through a very easy to use control panel. For those who do not want to wade through the different categories. There is an easier setup that allows you to choose the filtering level that meets your needs: low, medium, or high. The low filtering level blocks just adult content, where the high filtering level blocks adult content, social networking sites, video-sharing sites. and more. You can even set this up on your kids' Playstation, Wii, DS, Xbox, iPad, and even their iPhone.

- OpenDNS allows you to set up custom messages for your users to explain why you blocked a specific website. This kind of interaction with technology will help teach your kids how to develop safe Internet habits while they are learning how to use technology.

- Built in anti-fraud/phishing protection. OpenDNS automatically blocks websites known to be designed specifically for the purpose of committing fraud.

- OpenDNS provides an awesome report that will show you all the websites that have been blocked, which ones your users access the most, and they will notify of potential problems websites.

- You also get top-notch customer service whenever you have problems using OpenDNS.

Norton ConnectSafe for Home

This really is a free DNS service from a well-known Internet security company that also provides some filtering of unwanted content such as pornography, known unsafe websites, fraud, phishing, and infected websites, without installing any additional software.[10]

Norton ConnectSafe for Home gives you three levels of protection to choose from. All you need to do is change your default DNS IP address to the Norton ConnectSafe DNS IP address that corresponds to the level of protection/filtering you are interested in and immediately start enjoying the benefits of Enterprise level DNS Security for the home from a reputable Internet security company. No purchase necessary and no additional software is required.

The three levels of blocking/filtering are:

1. Security (malware, phishing sites and scam sites)

2. Security + Pornography

3. Security + Pornography + Other (non-family friendly content which includes sites that feature mature content, abortion, alcohol, crime, cult, drugs, gambling, hate, sexual orientation, suicide, tobacco or violence).

According to Norton's ConnectSafe for Home website you'll enjoy the following benefits from their service:

- Acts as a first layer of security by automatically blocking known unsafe websites set up or compromised by hackers and cyber criminals to commit fraud, collect information that can be used to steal an individual's identity or access banking accounts, etc.

- Protects your children from accessing undesirable content such as pornography

- After setting the level of protection you are interested in, it works in the background, doesn't affect your system's performance, and will protect all devices on your network in real time without any other changes.

If you are interested in simplicity then Norton ConnectSafe for Home is an excellent way of adding another layer of security to your home network without needing to learn how to configure settings.

I would rank Norton ConnectSafe above Google Public DNS, which we'll discuss next, because it provides you the added benefit of filtering/blocking without needing to install any other software or browser add-ins. My personal preference is still OpenDNS's commercial service ($19.95/year) because of the additional features such as reports, customized settings, black-lists, and white-lists, which you do not get with Norton's ConnectSafe for Home. However, ConnectSafe is an excellent option for anyone who doesn't want to play with settings and likes the "set it and forget it" option.

Google Public DNS & Comodo Secure DNS

If you are not interested in the filtering/blocking features of OpenDNS and Norton ConnectSafe for Home but would like to add a layer of security, then you might consider either Google Public DNS or Comodo Secure DNS. Most people are familiar with Google so it's not surprising they also provide a DNS service called Google Public DNS.[11], [12]

Comodo is a family of information technology security companies who also provide a free DNS service that helps protect you from some of the vulnerabilities in DNS. Neither Google Public DNS nor Comodo Secure DNS provide the same level of filtering/security you would get with OpenDNS or Norton ConnectSafe for Home, but they can improve your overall performance and provide some basic security benefits.

Step-by-step information is available for setting up Google Public DNS at https://developers.google.com/speed/public-dns/docs/using and for Comodo Secure DNS at http://www.comodo.com/secure-dns/index.html.

Google actually recommends users install a host-based filtering program or have a filter installed in your Internet browser. You will also find a list of browser plug-ins you might consider to help provide a filter against pornography and other types of malware in our chapter on hardening your Internet browser.

Image Searches

If you are trying to protect your children from accessing pornography, OpenDNS and Norton ConnectSafe for Home will do a good job of blocking pornographic websites. However, these services cannot block thumbnail images from being displayed in the image search features of sites like Google, Yahoo, and Bing.

This is a common problem discussed in online forums. There are other options you can use to ensure your children can only access age appropriate content. For example, according to Google there are two ways you can lock the safe search setting features of Google.

If you have a Google account, you can log in and lock the Safe-Search preferences. Keep in mind if your children have their own Google accounts they may be able to disable SafeSearch. See Google's documentation for setting up SafeSearch for more information. [13]

The second way you can enforce SafeSearch is by using a proxy server for your web traffic and configure the proxy's settings to append "&safe=strict" to all search requests sent to Google. This parameter enables strict SafeSearch for all searches, regardless of the setting on the Google Preferences page. This will filter out most of the offensive content but it is not foolproof.

Setting up a proxy server is a little more challenging than many of the recommendations I've discussed but it can be done easily if you have patience and take the time to learn. See the videos in appendix two for details on setting up a firewall such as pfSense or Sophos UTM for the home user. Alternatively there are some software solutions discussed in chapter three you can use as well.

Bing has a similar option.[14] The problem with any of these options is there are other ways to circumvent your settings, and as your children grow into teens they can become better and smarter at using the computer than you are and find ways to get around your security.

You can also lock down your computers by deciding which websites you'll allow your children to visit and then lock out all others by default. You can do this with OpenDNS by creating a white list of the approved websites. Any other websites would be blocked by default since they are not in the list of approved websites.

Yahoo once had a kid friendly search engine called Yahoo Kids but it was discontinued April 30, 2014.[15] Google does operate Safe-Search for Kids which is a good option for younger children, but as your children get older you'll want to explore other options.[16]

Summary

We wrap up this chapter on modems and routers with a summary of the best practices for routers you should consider to improve your overall security. The recurring theme you'll find throughout this book is adding layers of security.

I'm not aware of any solutions that will make you secure 100% of the time because for each security measure there is likely to be a counter-measure. Taking a layered approach to your security posture is the best way I know to improve your chances of not becoming a victim.

The following list of best practices is not all inclusive because as technology changes, threats and vulnerabilities also change. This may affect how we implement one or all of the recommendations. If you are using a method not addressed in this chapter that you believe will help other users, please participate in our forums. If it's something everyone can benefit from we will include your recommendation in our next revision and give you the credit for the suggestion.

The list is not in any order of precedence. You may decide to apply some, none, or all of the recommendations.

- Change the default user name and password for your router
- Create a network configuration document to use as your roadmap when making changes. The network configuration document will contain things like MAC addresses, make & model of specific devices on your network, the operating systems on each, white-list/black-list details etc. ***See appendix three for a sample network configuration document you can use as is or modify to suite your needs.
- Use a password to protect your network configuration document or store it in an encrypted folder to make sure only you or someone you trust can access it. Anyone with access to your network configuration document will have the keys to your kingdom.
- Create an access control list using a white-list or black-list

for your Ethernet connected devices depending on what is best for your situation/environment.

- Turn off your wireless access to your router if you are only using Ethernet connected devices.

- Implement wireless security if you are using wireless devices on your network by changing your SSID, setting-up encryption using WPA/WPA2.

- What to do about WPS?

  o Turn off WPS if it is available on your router. Research your specific router to see if it is vulnerable to the WPS attack described by Stefan Viehböck.

  o If your router is vulnerable to the WPS attack you might want to consider purchasing a router without WPS or see if one is available with WPS that has implemented mitigation for the WPS attack vulnerability.

- Consider setting up a white-list or black-list.

- Set up one of the free DNS Services described above that meets your goals.

- If you have children at home and do not want them exposed to pornography, then OpenDNS or Norton ConnectSafe for Home are your best DNS Service options.

References

[1] RouterPasswords.com. http://www.routerpasswords.com/

[2] Wikipedia contributors, "IEEE 802.11," Wikipedia, The Free Encyclopedia, http://en.wikipedia.org/w/index.php?title=IEEE_802.11&oldid=623438697

[3] Ajay Gupta. Broken WEP WiFi Encryption Still Operational in Large Numbers. Infosecurity Magazine. http://www.infosecurity-magazine.com/blogs/broken-wep-wifi-encryption-still-operational-in-la/

[4] Wi-Fi Alliance. Security. http://www.wi-fi.org/discover-wi-fi/security

[5] Tsitroulis, Achilleas, Dimitris Lampoudis, and Emmanuel Tsekleves. 2014. "Exposing WPA2 Security Protocol Vulnerabilities." International

Journal of Information and Computer Security 6 (1): 93. doi:10.1504/IJICS.2014.059797.

[6] Sean Gallagher. Hands-on: hacking WiFi Protected Setup with Reaver. Ars Technica. http://arstechnica.com/business/2012/01/hands-on-hacking-wifi-protected-setup-with-reaver/

[7] Stefan Viehböck. Brute Forcing WiFi Protected Setup – when poor design meets poor implementation. http://sviehb.files.wordpress.com/2011/12/viehboeck_wps.pdf

[8] James Fallows. Hacked. The Atlantic. http://www.theatlantic.com/magazine.archive/2011/11/hacked/308673/

[9] OpenDNS. Home Internet Security. OpenDNS. http://www.opendns.com/home-internet-security/

[10] Symantec Corporation. Norton ConnectSafe for Home. Symantec. https://dns.norton.com/homeuser.html

[11] Google Developers. Using Google Public DNS. Google. https://developers.google.com/speed/public-dns/docs/using

[12] Comodo Group, Inc. Comodo Secure DNS. Comodo Group, Inc. http://www.comodo.com/secure-dns/

[13] Google Developers. SafeSearch: Turn on or off. Google. https://support.google.com/websearch/answer/510?hl=en&ref_topic=3378866

[14] Microsoft. Block adult content with Safesearch. Microsoft. http://onlinehelp.microsoft.com/en-us/bing/ff808441.aspx

[15] Wikipedia contributors, "Yahoo! Kids," Wikipedia, The Free Encyclopedia, http://en.wikipedia.org/w/index.php?title=Yahoo!_Kids&oldid=623094598

[16] Google. Safe Search Kids. Google. http://www.safesearchkids.com/

CHAPTER THREE

SECURITY SOFTWARE

In this chapter I am going to discuss the different types of security software available so you can make an informed decision based upon your needs, resources, and maybe even your technical abilities. For the home user, we are going to look at five basic types of security software options available for your home network/computers: virus/malware protection, firewalls, Internet filters, all-in-one protection, and file/disk encryption.

There are almost as many free open source software options available as there are commercial products, and like so many things I'll discuss there are pros and cons for each. The most important thing is having protection for your network that meets your needs/goals. There are some good products that are available for free, but I really recommend you consider each option and make your decision based upon your situation.

Free is always nice, but free doesn't always mean best. Sometimes you might want to take a double barreled approach and use two different products for the same purpose, one free and one which costs because there isn't a software solution available that is a panacea solution for security.

The only exception to this double barreled approach would be with your firewall software. I do not recommend you use two different firewall programs on your computer because you are very likely to have conflicts. A better approach in this case would be to have a firewall setup on your router and one on your computer. Remember, once you've lost sensitive data because of a virus or malware, been hacked, or had your identity stolen, you will have to do a lot more work and possibly spend a lot of money to regain some control than if you take time now to learn basic steps that will help protect you.

Before I became interested in computer/network security, I hated when a new operating system came out because it almost always meant I had to spend some money to keep up with technology. When the budget is tight, you might take the approach I've heard many people take over the years, which is keep on keeping on with the system you have. Why fix something if it isn't broke?

Well, I have a different perspective these days because there are people in this world who are dedicated to stealing from others, and if you are using one of the older yet still popular operating systems you become more vulnerable with each passing day. This is because hackers and cyber criminals have more time to explore vulnerabilities in operating systems that are still in wide use.

Hackers and cyber criminals have more motivation to develop exploits for popular operating systems because more attack opportunities lead to higher success rates. With each passing day you become more vulnerable to being exploited when you access the Internet, even when you are using many of the principals outlined in this book. Don't give up hope though. You can improve your security.

If you are not using the Internet then you are not as vulnerable, but just about everyone I know is using the Internet and many elderly people are even active on online social networks like Facebook. One of the best practices you can take is to make sure you are using a modern operating system and that you are keeping it updated as the OS vendor releases security patches. You should also be doing this for any third party applications you are using. If the application does not have an automatic updater you should visit the vendor's website periodically to see if they have released security updates or patches.

Anti-Virus Software

Most people have a basic understanding of virus protection software but it can still be confusing. The first thing you need to remember is anti-virus software is not a cure all. You need to use anti-virus software along with other layers of security to ensure you have the best protection for your situation. In the article "Endpoint Protection" for the Dark reading web portal, author Robert Lemos reiterates that anti-virus protection should only be a part of your overall strategy.[1]

There are so many options and just as many vendors who claim to offer the best protection. What you select will depend on the operating system you're using because some vendors only make products for one operating system.

Do you have a Microsoft operating system, MAC, or Linux? Your operating system will likely be a major factor on your susceptibility and vulnerability to viruses and other malware. If you are a MAC or Linux user you may think you don't have anything to worry about, but you should think again. Microsoft products definitely have the greatest market share when it comes to exploitable vulnerabilities and malware. They are followed by MAC and then Linux. MAC OS users should remain cautious because as the user base grows, so too will the hackers and cyber criminals' motivation to tap into this generally unprotected market.

In the fall of 2011 there was a MAC OS X virus that infected more than 600,000 MAC systems globally. More than half of the infected systems were in the United States and 20% of the systems were in Canada.[2],[3]

Linux users also consider their OS as being impervious to viruses, but I still recommend you at least consider using some of the free antivirus programs that are available. I agree with most MAC and Linux users that they have a lower risk, but don't throw the baby out with the bath water when it comes to protecting your home network. There are always risks you can easily mitigate with a little preparation.

There is a growing number of OS independent malware that can be installed on your computer system merely by visiting a website because of software like Java.[4] Cyber criminals are also using other methods to distribute their malware, such as disguising it as a common product update like Adobe Reader® and relying on the user to accept the update as legitimate.[5]

Layers of security should be your new mantra. Look for products designed for your operating system, check out reviews, and make an informed decision. While there are probably some good small virus protection vendors out there I would almost always recommend you consider getting your virus protection software from a larger vendor because they generally have larger budgets and more resources to keep up with the latest threats and are able to quickly develop signatures to detect and mitigate new viruses. Some security experts estimate there are more than 250,000 new malware variants detected daily and more than 30,000 websites exploited daily. These numbers are staggering.

In the last few years Microsoft developed the Microsoft Security Essentials program as a free add-on for use with Windows Vista, and Windows 7 to help protect against viruses, malware, spyware, and other malicious software. The features available in Microsoft Security essentials are built in to Windows 8, which gives Windows 8 users' protection out of the box instead of requiring users to download Microsoft Security Essentials or to find a third party vendor. [6]

I personally prefer virus protection software from some of the larger security vendors such as Norton and McAfee but there are many other options. PC Magazine reviews virus protection software annually; their review includes details about the different free virus protection software available as well. According to PC Magazine: "No budget for security? That's no excuse for skipping antivirus protection. With 9.3 points for malware blocking, AVG Anti-Virus FREE 2013 scored better than both Bitdefender and Norton, and its malware removal score of 6.5 points took third place, behind Norton and Webroot. AVG is our current Editors' Choice for free antivirus." See appendix two in the back of the book for links to all the vendors' websites mentioned by PC Magazine's annual review of virus protection software. You can find PC Magazine's annual article for 2013 by using the following string in quotes with your favorite search engine: "The Best Antivirus for 2013."

If you suspect you have a virus but your anti-virus software has not detected a problem, you should try scanning your system with another anti-virus tool or use one of the online virus scanners highlighted in the next section. If you are using a Microsoft-based system, I recommend you periodically run the Microsoft Malicious Software Removal Tool.[7] Microsoft releases an update of this very useful tool on the second Tuesday of each month. At a minimum you should run it once a month or more often if your system begins acting strange. It is not intended to be your anti-virus software solution because it does not run in the background constantly looking for a virus like anti-virus suites/software. It is designed to be downloaded periodically and run as needed to remove some pretty nasty malware. It's best to download it and let it run without interrupting the scan or using your computer.

Microsoft also provides an on-demand scanner in addition to the Malicious Software Removal Tool you can download. According to Microsoft the "Microsoft Safety Scanner" is meant to be used alongside your existing antivirus program. The scanner engine expires 10 days after its downloaded so you need to download it routinely for maximum benefit.[8]

Online Virus Scanners

Many virus protection software vendors also provide an online scanner that doesn't cost anything and gives you the benefit of scanning your system with different detection engines without needing to purchase any additional software. These online virus scanners may require a small application or browser plug-in to be installed on your computer to work.

A quick online search will find a number of different online virus scanners such as BitDefender, Computer Associates Malware Scanner, ESET online malware scanner, NanoScan by Panda Software, McAfee FreeScan, Avast, TrendMicro, etc.

These should not be considered as replacements for virus protection software because they do not provide protection all the time like software running in the background on your computer. I recommend them because they do offer some benefits if you are trying to rid yourself of a particularly pesky malware your current virus protection software has not been able to remove. See appendix one in the back of the book for links to many of the online virus scanners available on the Internet.

Firewalls

Firewalls are just as essential as virus protection software and they are usually installed on the perimeter of a network. The name should give you a good idea of what it is designed to do because it's analogous to a brick firewall in a building that is designed as a barrier to keep fire from spreading between different areas of a building.

Many of today's home use routers have a stateful packet inspection (SPI) along with Network Address Translation (NAT) enabled straight out of the box. The SPI firewall is designed to keep track of all transactions into and out of your network. It will allow the computers and other devices on your network to initiate a transaction (visit a website, check email, start a chat session, stream a video from Netflix, etc.), and it will keep track of the session as long as it is active. It will block any transactions that are initiated from the Internet, which is one of the primary benefits of a firewall.

If your computer is connected to the Internet using only a modem, then you really should have a host-based (computer application firewall) or a separate computer setup as a firewall to help protect your computer.

All versions of Microsoft Windows since Windows XP have the Windows Firewall program and, unless you install another firewall program, you should have it turned on for protection. There are three basic settings: on (this is the recommended setting); on/block all incoming connections (used when you need extra security because you are using your computer on a public network or for when a worm is spreading across the Internet); or off (not recommended unless you have another program installed or have an SPI firewall on your router).[9]

Many of today's Internet security suites have a firewall application included. When you install one of these suites you should turn off Windows Firewall to ensure there are no conflicts between the two firewall programs.

MAC OS X also has an application firewall available for v10.5 and later.[10] The features are almost identical between the two different versions (v10.5 vs v10.6 >) but configuring them are slightly different. Once the application firewall is turned on, there are three options found under the "Advanced" settings: block all incoming connections (this applies to all connections except a few services essential to the operating system); automatically allow signed software to receive incoming connections (this feature will allow all applications that are digitally signed by Apple to make connections without the user needing to allow the connection. Apple iTunes service is an example of a service that would be allowed to connect because it has a digital certificate signed by Apple); and enable stealth mode (the computer will not respond to connection requests or reply to ICMP (ping) requests although it will still respond to digitally signed/authorized applications.)

An authorized application is one that may not have an Apple digital certificate, but the user has made a decision to allow this application to receive incoming connections. The application firewall will digitally sign an application and add it to the allow list or deny list depending on how the user responded to the dialog for the application.

For users who like to explore other options, there are several Linux firewalls that can be configured and set up on an older computer with two network interface cards. One of the cards is connected to your modem and the other is connected to the Internet port on your router. According to Martin Meredith in an article for the Linux Format magazine there are several excellent Linux firewalls that are very easy to set up and include a lot of features not found on most home use firewalls.[11]

Internet Filter & Accountability Software

Internet filter software provides many of the same features we discussed in Chapter two with the different DNS based Internet filtering services. The primary difference between an Internet filter program and the DNS based Internet filtering is where the service resides on your network. It is a program installed on your computer, whereas the DNS based Internet filtering is a service you do not install on your computer but configure through your router or through your network interface card.

Just like all the security options you might consider after re-searching some of the suggestions presented in this book, there are pros and cons for each.

Internet Filtering Software	Internet Filtering through DNS
Must be installed on each computer to be protected	Protects all computers connected to the network.
Licenses may be limited (1 – 3 PCs). Additional licenses cost more money.	Protects the network rather than by the hosts so no additional costs to protect more PCs.
Easier to disable and bypass	More difficult to disable and bypass
Must be routinely updated on each machine	Updates are transparent and done by the DNS service provider
Does not work if a live CD is booted for temporary use	Continues to work even if a live CD is booted for temporary use
Is OS dependent; may not be available for your OS.	Is not OS dependent; works with all versions of OS.
May or may not be easy to setup	Usually more challenging to setup

Fortunately, or unfortunately depending on how you look at it, the options for Internet filtering software are going to make choosing one for your situation a little easier because there are only a few competitive packages due to the smaller market segment for this type of software.

Businesses are more likely to choose Internet filtering as a service or will have a hardware appliance that sits on their network like a router to perform filtering for different reasons than the home user. A home user may decide to take a double barreled approach and use a software-based filtering program along with a DNS-based filtering service and achieve a high degree of success without a lot of investment in time or money.

One thing to keep in mind. Internet filtering software suffers from the same challenges as DNS based Internet filtering services. They cannot completely block all explicit images, especially when you use a search engine's image search tool. What can you do to help counter this weakness? If you think or know you can get away with something you may be tempted to try. Many teenagers who have grown up using computers and the Internet are very resourceful and learn how to circumvent filtering software. This is where accountability software comes into our discussion.

Accountability software is usually a separate program from an Internet filtering software package. This kind of software does not protect the user from any kind of explicit material. Instead, this kind of software gives those who use it the motivation to stay away from certain types of activities because they do not want to disappoint their accountability partner, who may be a parent, a friend, a counselor, or a spouse.

This kind of software works by keeping track of different kinds of activity on a computer. Not all software packages provide the same features, but they all work by keeping track of certain activity such as logging Internet search terms, sites visited, instant message activity, etc., and emailing your accountability partner when there is a violation of the software's parameters.

On some packages, the activity results in an immediate email to your accountability partner, in other cases it's a daily or weekly email of all activity, or it may require the accountability partner to log into a dashboard online to view the others Internet activity. This kind of software has its roots in addiction recovery and can be very useful to help users keep themselves away from addictive activity. This type of software is available for all kinds of devices, including many mobile devices and smart phones.

While Internet filtering is a small market segment there are a lot of options. I ran across the iboss Home by Phantom Technologies Inc. while researching this topic. The iboss Home does not really fit into the Internet filtering software category completely, nor does it fit into the DNS Internet filtering as a service category. This is a hardware solution along with an annual subscription similar to OpenDNS. I have not had a chance to test it but the concept is solid and it seems well supported. [12]

I wanted to highlight this particular provider because their literature said they are able to enforce safe search on Google, Bing, Ya-hoo, Ask and others, even if it's disabled in the browser. According to information on the iboss Home website: "Just one iboss Home protects all computers and devices that access the Internet in your house and provides the ease of centrally managing these devices. The iboss Home combines a multi-tiered approach, advanced layer 7 filtering, deep packet inspection and signature analysis as well a hardened Linux firewall and Wireless-N router. The iboss Home Parental Control Router provides a hardware-based, single and flexible solution to manage all Internet access in your home."

From the description, this particular product provides a lot of features at a reasonable price. Just replace your current router with the iboss Home wireless router and subscribe to the service to protect all the devices on your network with individually definable filtering options and a hardened Linux firewall. This type of appliance is traditionally marketed to a much larger audience (schools, mid-size business, government organizations, etc).

Because the iboss Home is a combination device/service, it will not impact the performance of your computers because nothing has to be installed on your computers. It will apply the same filtering technology to all devices regardless of the operating system (Windows, MAC, Linux, or game console).

There is one other type of software you might consider if you are dealing with adolescent/teenage children, and it's basically spy software you can install on most cell phones/smart phones. One example is Stealth Genie that can be used to keep track of phone call data (numbers called/received), read SMS traffic (sent/received), track GPS data, read web-based email (sent/received), view multimedia files on the device, remotely activate the phone's speaker and listen to conversations going on near the phone, track Internet activities, and many other features.

I'm not recommending this kind of software be used in secret but instead use it as you would accountability software. Full disclosure of what can be monitored is probably sufficient for most situations to change or temper someone's behavior.

All-in-One Suites

If trying to fine-tune several software packages for your network security doesn't sound like a lot of fun, then you may want to consider trying an all-in-one suite. There are several vendors who provide all-in-one suites that really make adding security to your computer and home network a lot easier than it once was.

The features for these suites vary like all things, so it may be a good idea to choose an all-in-one suite that has a large user base/market share in the business enterprise market. When choosing an all-in-one suite, I recommend looking at what it provides: anti-virus, Internet filtering, firewall, email scanning, parental controls, social networking protection, and encryption options for sensitive data at a minimum. A larger company should be able to keep up with the constantly changing threat landscape because they generally have a larger research and development budget. Many of the anti-virus/firewall product links we've provided in appendix one also have all-in-one products.

Encryption Software

I want to finish this chapter by briefly looking at encryption software and discussing why you should consider using it. Fortunately, most of today's newest operating systems include basic encryption options by default. In cases where your operating system does not include encryption there are options in both open source software and commercial software markets.

Why would you want to encrypt anything on your personal computer? I hear of people all the time who say they do not have any sensitive data on their computers and don't need any encryption. These same people also do their taxes on their computer, work from home for their company, they may even do their personal finances, and very likely even have a file or two with their or their spouses Social Security number or similar personally identifiable information on their computer.

What if all this data is on their laptop or smart phone and it is stolen? Without any encryption protection, anyone who can physically access the storage device will be able to access all this sensitive information.

How you implement encryption is just as important as the decision to use it. With today's computers there can be terabytes of storage available so you do not need to encrypt everything. I recommend using an implementation strategy where you store your sensitive information in encrypted folders and/or disks that are separate from your operating system. This will give you peace of mind in situations where you need to have your computer serviced or in situations where your laptop and/or computer are stolen.

An external USB memory stick, solid state drive, or hard drive is perfect for this situation. USB memory sticks are now available in sizes up to 128GB for less than $100, which is perfect for protecting your sensitive information. Even in cases where you don't use an external storage device, you can use a second internal drive and remove it before turning your computer in for service. Many people will shy away from using encryption software because it sounds too complicated. It's actually very simple to set up encryption, and there are many options.

The CNSS fact sheet on the Advanced Encryption System (AES) published in June 2003 claimed the design and strength of all key lengths of the AES algorithm (i.e., 128, 192 and 256) are sufficient to protect classified information up to the SECRET level. TOP SECRET information requires either the 192 or 256 key lengths. Many of the products available today implement AES. So if the encryption is good enough for classified government information, then it provides and outstanding level of protection for the home or small business user.

If you are using a Microsoft Windows product and want to use the Microsoft products that allow you to encrypt files and/or partitions you have two options. The earliest product developed by Microsoft is the Encrypting File System (EFS) which is available for use on Windows 2000, Windows XP Professional, and Windows Server 2003. It is not available for the Windows XP Home operating system.

The newest product developed by Microsoft is the BitLocker® Drive Full-volume Encryption available for use on Vista Professional and later desktop operating systems, and Windows Server 2008 and later for servers. There are differences between how EFS is implemented in the Windows 2000, XP and Server 2003. The best source of information on the differences and how to use these products (EFS & BitLocker® Drive Full-volume Encryption) is the Microsoft Windows and Microsoft Technet websites.[13],[14]

If you are using a MAC with OS X 10.3 or later then you can use FileVault, which can encrypt your home directory, individual folders, complete disks, and even removable drives. FileVault only uses 128-AES for encryption but this shouldn't give you any reason to doubt its effectiveness or strength.[15]

AES as a whole is the best encryption standard available for consumers or businesses. Linux users are not left out in the cold either and many of the most popular Linux distributions have provided the option to encrypt your home directories for several years now.

All the options we discussed so far are for files stored locally on your computer or on external storage devices. If you are accustomed to using storage in the cloud then you can still protect your data using AES-256 encryption in the cloud.

One such product available for use with many of the most common cloud providers is BoxCryptor. I have not personally tried Box-Cryptor and would caution anyone who uses a cloud storage option to only store sensitive data on a device for which they personally control. If however, you choose to use a cloud storage provider for your data, then BoxCryptor may be a good option for you. There are two versions of BoxCryptor you can choose from. BoxCryptor FREE and BoxCryptor Unlimited Personal. The only difference is the free version is limited to only one encrypted drive and does not give you file name encryption.[16]

Precautions with Encryption

This header is meant to get your attention without causing you to contemplate not using encryption. I want to emphasize how important using encryption can be for your personal security program. The best security is implemented in layers and encryption is one layer worth investing your time into learning more about. There are some basic best practices I want you to consider as you develop a strategy that meets your needs.

Your password is your lifeline to your encrypted files, folders, or volumes. You need a good, complex password that will be resistant to a brute force dictionary attack in case your encrypted media is stolen.

Share your password with your spouse or have it locked in a safe deposit box they have access to if something happens to you. This will save them a lot of trouble in an already difficult situation and can also save you a lot of frustration and trouble if you forget your password.

None of the encryption software programs mentioned have a back door. If you forget your password and did not store it somewhere safe such as a safe deposit box then you will not be able to access your encrypted files.

Backup, backup, backup! Encrypted files, folders, and drives can become corrupted just like any other file system. You should have a backup of your data in case your encrypted data becomes corrupted and cannot be recovered.

Choose an encryption program that meets your needs and is easy to use. If the program is so complex that using it is difficult then you will probably stop using it.

Summary

The most important take away from this chapter is layers of security. Each layer you add will improve your overall protection. The best "best practice" I can recommend is make sure you implement most of these recommendations.

Nothing listed here will protect you completely but the more you do to change your habits by routinely thinking about protecting your network, your family, and your personal information, the more you'll learn and change your habits.

Trust me, the hackers and cyber criminals are constantly thinking about how they can take advantage of unsuspecting/unprotected people using the Internet. If you believe the threat is real then you will be more likely to take steps to protect yourself. Consider just a few of the following headlines:

'Red October' Attacks: The New Face Of Cyberespionage, Jan 14, 2013[17]

Two-Thirds of Banks Hit By Cyberattack In Past 12 Months, Jan 22, 2013[18]

Study Finds More Than 10,000 ID Fraud Rings In the U.S., Nov 14, 2012[19]

Ransomware Scams Net $5 Million Per Year, Nov 8, 2012[20]

Majority Of South Carolinians' Social Security Numbers Exposed In Hack, Oct 29, 2012[21]

On an average day there are 250,000 new malware variants and more than 30,000 websites compromised, Apr 25, 2013[22]

References

[1] Lemos, Robert. 2014. "Endpoint Security." *Dark Reading*. Accessed September 7. http://www.darkreading.com/end-user/endpoint-security/240155825

[2] Musil, Steven. 2012. "More than 600,000 Macs Infected with Flashback Botnet." *CNET*, April 4. http://www.cnet.com/news/more-than-600000-macs-infected-with-flashback-botnet/

[3] Newcomb, Alyssa. 2012. "Mac OS X Report: Virus Infects 600,000 Computers." *ABC News Blogs*. http://abcnews.go.com/blogs/technology/2012/04/mac-os-x-report-virus-infects-600000-computers/

[4] Dunn, John. 2014. "CryptoDefense Ransom Malware Using Java Drive-by Exploit to Boost Infection Rate." *Techworld*, May 27. http://news.techworld.com/security/3521777/cryptodefense-ransom-malware-using-java-drive-by-exploit-to-boost-infection-rate/

[5] Cluley, Graham. 2011. "Beware Adobe Software Upgrade Notification - Malware Attached!" *Naked Security*. http://nakedsecurity.sophos.

com/2011/12/06/beware-adobe-software-upgrade-notification-mal-ware-attached/

[6] "Microsoft Security Essentials - Microsoft Windows." 2014. *Windows.microsoft.com*. http://windows.microsoft.com/en-us/windows/security-essentials-download

[7] Microsoft. 2014. "Free Malware Removal Tool | Anti-Malware Scan Software." http://www.microsoft.com/security/pc-security/malware-removal.aspx

[8] Microsoft. 2014. "Microsoft Safety Scanner - Free Virus Scan with the Microsoft Safety Scanner." http://www.microsoft.com/security/scanner/en-us/default.aspx

[9] "Understanding Windows Firewall Settings - Windows Help." 2014. *Windows.microsoft.com*. http://windows.microsoft.com/en-us/windows/understanding-firewall-settings

[10] Apple Inc. 2014. "OS X: About the Application Firewall." http://support.apple.com/kb/ht1810.

[11] Martin Meredith. 7 of the best Linux firewalls http://www.techradar.com/us/news/software/applications/7-of-the-best-linux-firewalls-697177#articleContent

[12] "Iboss Network Security – Web Security, Mobile Security, and Advanced Threat and Data Protection for Today's Borderless Network." 2014. http://residential.iphantom.com/

[13] "Windows BitLocker Drive Encryption Step-by-Step Guide." 2007. http://technet.microsoft.com/en-us/library/c61f2a12-8ae6-4957-b031-97b4d762cf31

[14] "What Is Encrypting File System (EFS)? - Windows Help." 2014. Windows.microsoft.com. http://windows.microsoft.com/en-us/windows/what-is-encrypting-file-system

[15] "OS X: About FileVault 2." 2014. http://support.apple.com/kb/HT4790

[16] "Boxcryptor | Encryption for Cloud Storage | Window, Mac, Android, iOS." 2014. https://www.boxcryptor.com/

[17] Higgins, Kelly Jackson. 2013. "'Red October' Attacks: The New Face Of Cyberespionage." Dark Reading. http://www.darkreading.com/attacks-breaches/red-october-attacks-the-new-face-of-cybe/240146237

[18] Dark Reading. 2013. "Two-Thirds of Banks Hit By Cyberattack In Past 12 Months," http://www.darkreading.com/attacks-breaches/two-thirds-of-banks-hit-by-cyberattack-i/240146738

[19] Dark Reading. 2012. "Study finds more than 10,000 ID fraud rings in the U.S." http://www.darkreading.com/identity-and-access-management/167901114/security/attacks-breaches/240134973/study-finds-more-than-10-000-id-fraud-rings-in-the-u-s.html

[20] Dark Reading. 2012. "Ransomeware scans net 5 million per year" http://www.darkreading.com/insider-threat/167801100/security/attacks-breaches/240062694/ransomware-scams-net-5-million-per-year.html

[21] Dark Reading. 2012. "Majority of South Carolinians Social Security Numbers Exposed In Hack." http://www.darkreading.com/database-security/167901020/security/attacks-breaches/240012534/majority-of-south-carolinians-social-security-numbers-exposed-in-hack.html

[22] Field, Tom. 2013. "Cyber-Attacks: The New Maturity." *Bank Info Security*. http://www.bankinfosecurity.com/interviews/cyber-attacks-new-maturity-i-1898.

Chapter Four

Physical Security

A chapter on physical security may seem out of place in a book focused on network and Internet security. Physical security is given equal emphasis in the military and in many large organizations because you cannot secure what you do not control. It's worth taking a little time to consider how physical security can protect your investment in information technology. You may be surprised to find some of the information in this chapter is a little more technical than you might expect but it's worth your time to learn about physical security.

We'll look at a few aspects of physical security you may want to consider during the lifetime of your computer systems, such as physical controls, technical controls, theft protection, and protection during power related anomalies (blackout/brownout), as well as steps you can take to protect your information after your computer system has served its usefulness.

External Hard Drive/USB memory

One of the easiest ways to protect your important data is to use an external hard drive for saving all your documents and data files. It's very easy to implement this type of security without needing to use any kind of special software or technology.

The key to ensuring your data remains protected from remote users over the Internet is to disconnect the external drive or USB memory device anytime you are connected to the Internet. This does take a little discipline but it will help ensure your data cannot be easily downloaded if you are infected (unknowingly) with malware

51

capable of sending data from infected hosts. Let's look at a few different ways this can be done.

- Physically disconnect your external hard drive's USB, Ethernet, or WiFi connection before you connect to the Internet
- Power down your external hard drive before you connect to the Internet
- Mount/connect your external hard drive using your OS when you are not connected to the Internet
- Physically remove your USB memory device before you connect to the Internet

These are only a few ways of ensuring you protect your important data and help keep it away from hackers.

Data Erasure for Reuse

What do you do when your computer system is getting old and you are worried about the data on your computer's hard drive falling into the wrong hands? What about backups on CDs, DVDs, solid state drives (SDD), flash memory (USB drives, micro SD, etc)? Well, if you took the advice discussed in our chapter on security software and are using encryption software then your sensitive data should be well protected even if your hard drive or other storage media fails.

Encryption is one of the best safeguards an individual can use to help prevent their data from falling into the wrong hands. I cannot emphasize the importance of using encryption enough.

You cannot simply delete the information or reformat the drive because of the way data is stored on a hard drive or other storage device. When you delete a file, all you've actually done is delete the pointer used by the computer's file system to locate the data. The data is still on the storage media and can be recovered until it has actually been overwritten in some way or you are able to execute a secure erase.

One other challenge when using flash memory or SDDs is related to how data is actually stored. There are significant differences in how each type of storage device operates and these differences affect how they are purged of data for reuse, or the steps needed to physically destroy them.

If you are using a personal computer that has ATA/IDE drives, which includes PATA and SATA drives made since 2001, you should be able to use "Secure Erase" (SE). SE is described as a "positive easy-to-use data destroy command, amounting to "electronic data shredding." [1][2]

SE is a simple addition to the existing "format drive" command present in computer operating systems and storage system software, and adds no cost to hard disk drives. Since the Secure Erase command is carried out within a hard disk drive, it doesn't require any additional software to implement.

You can download the command line tool used to execute the commands stored on each IDE/SCSI device and execute SE to prepare your hard drives for reuse or complete destruction. Gordon Hughes & Tom Coughlin developed an excellent tutorial on disk drive sanitization just about anyone can use.[2]

If you have a MAC OS X 10.2.3 or later, you can use the Disk Utility to securely erase a hard disk. The steps to erase a hard disk can be found on the Apple support website and when used in conjunction with encryption will provide a relatively secure method of sanitizing/purging a MAC OS X hard disk.

You should definitely use this tool if you decide to sell your system with the existing hard drive. For complete peace of mind it would be best to use the Disk Utility to erase the data on the drive, and then physically destroy it by other means and sell the system without the hard drive.[3]

If you have an SDD, USB, or other flash memory, the SE commands may not work or only result in partial erasure of the information on the device. The tools needed to securely erase these types of deices are not standardized as in the case of IDE devices. Each device is different depending on the manufacturer.

The best thing you can do when using these types of drives/storage devices is to use encryption and a method of physical destruction you are comfortable with. Some manufacturers of these types of devices have included commands or tools to securely erase them but each produces different results under testing.

Michael Wei, Laura M. Grupp, Frederick E. Spada, and Steven Swanson of the University of California, San Diego and the Center for Magnetic Recording Research (CMRR) wrote a paper based on their research into reliably erasing data from flash-based solid state devices that is worth reading to better understand the challenges with purging data stored on these types of devices.[4]

Free Clearing/Purging Software

If you have a Windows-based computer and only need to delete individual files or directories then you might try using "Eraser", which is one of the tools Peter Gutmann recommends.[5]

According to the Eraser website, "Eraser is an advanced security tool for Windows which allows you to completely remove sensitive data from your hard drive by overwriting it several times with carefully selected patterns. Eraser is currently supported under Windows XP (with Service Pack 3), Windows Server 2003 (with Service Pack 2), Windows Vista, Windows Server 2008, Windows 7 and Windows Server 2008 R2." Eraser can be downloaded from the Sourceforge project page.[6]

Another tool for Microsoft Windows-based systems is the HD-DErase.exe program. It has not been updated since 2008 but it is still an effective tool. HDDErase.exe was developed by the CMRR for the National Security Agency and is designed to securely erase (sanitizes) everything on ATA hard disk drives for computers based on the Intel architecture.

You may shy away from using DOS-based utilities, but there is an easy to follow user guide that walks you through the process step by step.[7] It allows you to use the hard drive's internal secure erase command.

If you want to erase a complete hard drive (not SSD or Flash memory), then you may want to try Derik's Boot and Nuke (DBAN), which can be installed on a USB memory stick or on a CD/DVD.

The DBAN website provides detailed instructions on how to install DBAN and get it up and running. Once you have it installed, you'll be able to boot to the CD/DVD or memory stick you used when installing DBAN. Ensure you read all the instructions before you use DBAN, or you may wipe a drive you don't want erased.[8]

The Linux shred command is available for anyone using a Linux distribution. It can also be used to delete a hard drive, but be prepared to wait a long time for it to complete the job if you have a large hard drive. Once Shred has overwritten the hard drive you'll need to reformat it before you can use it again.[9]

Commercial Clearing/Purging Software

If you want a guarantee-backed software package for deleting your sensitive data files, you can also try Blanco PC Edition for whole disk erasing and Blanco File for individual files. The Blanco PC Edition and Blanco File are both available as a download/purchase from the Blanco online store for approximately $30.00.[10]

Physical Destruction

The heading says it all. There are a lot of different ways you might destroy a hard drive, SSD, USB memory drive, other flash memory or a CD/DVD disk. It all depends on what you have available and how much work you want to put into destroying your drives.

One of the easiest ways to physically destroy a hard drive after you've erased the data is to use a drill and put a few holes through it. If you've got access to a drill press, then clamp it down and drill three or four holes through the drive. You can disassemble some drives down to the platters if you are concerned that just putting a few holes through the drive is not enough. If you disassemble a drive, you may be able to independently destroy the platters using an angle grinder. For USB memory sticks, a vice and a hand drill works well. One or two holes should do the trick.

An oxygen/acetylene torch is another option you can use to destroy a hard drive. This method doesn't take a lot of effort and is a good way to ensure complete destruction if you've got access to a torch.

If you enjoy smashing things with a sledge hammer then doing so is another effective way to render most hard drives, SSDs, and other USB memory devices unusable.

Laptop/Smart Phone Theft

Laptops and smart phones are portable by design, which can make their theft a lot easier than a desktop. If you implement encryption and require accounts with complex passwords, as suggested throughout this book, you can rest easy knowing your data will be safe if it is stolen.

If you decide not to use encryption then you might be interested in anti-theft software in case your laptop or smart phone is stolen. They should probably call this kind of software theft recovery, anti-identity theft, or anti-data theft software because it does not deter a theft from happening.

In fact, in some cases the software is intentionally hidden to keep a thief from disabling it so you will be able to find it and remote into your system when the thief connects it to the Internet. The software may help you recover your laptop using a GPS tracker or other method using the IP address to determine the systems approximate location.

This kind of software may allow you to remotely delete sensitive data or encrypt the contents of your drives to protect your information. It does nothing to keep someone from stealing your laptop or smart phone, but can give you peace of mind if it is stolen.

Uninterrupted Power Supply

Power surges or an unexpected loss of power can result in damage to your hard drives or computer's motherboard/chips. Uninterrupted power supplies have a battery that is ready to provide a few minutes of power if you lose power. They can protect your computer from these types of power issues and may save you hundreds of dollars in damages to your computer.

Most uninterrupted power supplies have two banks of plugs:

- Power surges protection bank
- Battery-backed power bank in case of power loss

You should plug your computer and monitor into the battery-backed power bank and your other devices (modem, router) into the power surge bank.

If you use a laser printer, you should plug it into a separate outlet/power strip. Do not use your uninterrupted power supply for your laser printer. If you do, you may cause it to fail and result in damage to your computer.[11]

References

[1] Center for Magnetic Recording Research. Secure Erase. Secure Erase. http://cmrr.ucsd.edu/people/Hughes/SecureErase.shtml

[2] Gordon Hughes and Tom Coughlin. Tutorial on Disk Drive Data Sanitization. http://cmrr.ucsd.edu/people/Hughes/DataSanitizationTutorial.pdf

[3] Apple Inc. Keeping your confidential data secure during hardware repair. http://support.apple.com/kb/HT3294

[4] Michael Wei, Laura M. Grupp, Frederick E. Spada, and Steven Swanson. Reliably Erasing Data From Flash-Based Solid State Drives. https://db.usenix.org/events/fast11/tech/full_papers/Wei.pdf

[5] Peter Gutmann. Secure Deletion of Data from Magnetic and Solid-State Memory. http://www.cs.auckland.ac.nz/~pgut001/pubs/secure_del.html

[6] Garrett Trant, Joel Low, and Sami Tolvanen. Eraser. http://sourceforge.net/projects/eraser/

[7] Center for Magnetic Recording Research. HDDErase.exe User Guide. http://cmrr.ucsd.edu/people/Hughes/HDDEraseReadMe.txt

[8] Dariks Boot and Nuke. http://www.dban.org/

[9] Colin Plumb. Linux Shred Command Man Page. http://linux.die.net/man/1/shred

[10] Blancco Oy Ltd. Blancco PC Edition. http://www.blancco.com/us/products/total-data-erasure/pc-edition/

[11] American Power Conversion Corporation. User Manual, APC Smart-UPS® SC. http://www.apcmedia.com/salestools/ASTE-6Z8LTZ/ ASTE-6Z8LTZ_R2_EN.pdf

Chapter Five

Operating System Security

I once followed the recommendations I heard my grandparents say time and again, and applied it to my use of computers, "if it isn't broke, then don't fix it."

Before we even talk about making your OS a bit more secure than how it comes configured out of the box, I want to give you some advice that is different than my grandparents. If you are using an outdated OS and you are connecting to the Internet, then you really need to upgrade.

I cannot believe how many individuals and organizations I run across who are still using Windows XP, which is no longer supported. The cost of upgrading keeps coming down and you can get a new computer with a modern and currently supported OS. Upgrading to a new computer/operating system will help ensure you are protected against vulnerabilities that are mitigated by routinely installing security patches.

Everything I recommend to enhance your security is about adding layers of security. While there are a lot of very good products that claim to provide the best security for home users there are no cure all's. Good security is applied in layers and this should be your goal.

We've already talked about securing your network boundary at the router and the different security software packages. Your computer's operating system security should also be tightened up a bit to help add another layer to your overall security and enhance your protection.

Regardless of the OS you use, there are common best practices applicable to all and other more specific steps you can take for your individual operating system. We'll discuss the common steps you can take for most operating systems and then focus on other steps applicable to securing specific operating systems.[1]

You can choose to employ all, some, or none of these suggestions, but the important thing is to know what you can do to improve your security and why these steps are important.

While researching this book I was discouraged to find Home versions of the Windows Operating Systems (OS) do not allow you to set advanced security features.[2], [3], [4] Home users represent the largest segment of users, yet they are usually provided with the least secure Windows operating systems.

You can still implement most of the best practices discussed in this chapter. However, you are limited in how your Windows OS can be configured. For example, you can set a complex password, but you cannot enforce complex passwords for all accounts, which means if you have other members of your family or organization using your computer and they are not using a good password then your security is at greater risk. Granted, the risk may be minimal, but you should minimize risk whenever possible.

If you can afford to upgrade to one of the Professional or Ultimate versions of the Windows OS, you will have more control over security settings. While upgrading is not always popular because it costs money, there are very good reasons you may want to consider upgrading.

Many people ask, why pay for an upgrade when what you have works? My personal recommendation is balanced: upgrade to a professional version of Windows if you can afford it. If your computer will support the latest version of Windows OS, then upgrade to that. If you are using Windows XP or earlier and your computer will not support one of the newer versions of Windows, then I'd recommend you get a new computer, never connect it to the Internet, or upgrade to a version of Linux that will run on your computer and provide better options for securing your computer. There are many how-to guides about installing Linux. See the reference to this chapter for an excellent article on installing Linux.[5]

Common Best Practices

User Accounts – One of the first things you need to do is create separate user accounts that do not have system administrator privileges and use them for your day-to-day computing. When you surf the Internet, check your email, or use other social networking applications like Skype, Facebook, or Google+ with elevated privileges (administrator/super user), you are at a greater risk from attacks that take advantage of user accounts running with elevated privileges. I'm not going to discuss the details about each of the specific types of attacks at this time, but I want to encourage you to read more about these risks.

When you surf the Internet and are required to enter data in a form or are logging into a website, you become susceptible to cross site scripting attacks (XSS).[6]

When you click on a website link sent via email, you could be susceptible to an XSS attack.

When you open an email with an attachment you may inadvertently allow malicious software to be installed without your knowledge.

When you chat with others using Skype, Facebook, Google+ or other social networking application files passed between users may contain malicious software that can automatically be installed on your computer.

The only time you should use your administrator account is to create other accounts, install software, perform operating system updates, and do other routine system administration tasks that cannot be done using a standard user account, and if at all possible you should do so only when you are not connected to the Internet.

The exception is when you are performing operating system or third party application updates that require access to the Internet. One way to avoid using the Internet with your administrator account for system updates is to download the updates using your non-privileged account and then running the updates with your administrator account.

Windows operating systems will also allow you to right click on the file you are installing or updating and select the option to install or run as the administrator. Once you've selected this option, you'll be prompted for your administrator password to confirm you want to run the program.

Guest Accounts. I personally don't believe guest accounts are necessary for a home computer, but they are there by default on Windows, Mac, and many versions of the Linux OS. Most OS guest accounts are disabled by default, but you should check the status of your guest accounts.

If they are enabled, then you should disable them unless you are currently using them and monitoring their use. Guest accounts usually do not require a password, provide access to your network, and in some operating systems can be used by others remotely.

If an attacker can log into a guest account, they have a starting point to launch attacks that may take advantage of any software vulnerabilities they find on your system in order to gain administrator access. Once they have administrator access, they now own your system and can pretty much do anything you can.

If you still believe you need a guest account, then disable the default guest account, create one with a different name, and set a good password. Speaking of passwords, we'll look at password enforcement next.

Password enforcement. This is one of first things you should do after making your user accounts. Require all users to have a password. If your operating system allows the system administrator to require complex passwords, along with setting minimum password length, then I'd recommend you take that extra step and require complex passwords at least eight characters long. I personally like complex passwords that are no less than 12 characters in length.

I really hate the term password because by context it implies you use a word in response to the challenge or login prompt. I believe we should use the term pass-code which sounds like something that would be challenging for a hacker to break or guess.

If you think about passwords differently, you might choose to create one that is not susceptible to a dictionary attack, which would make it harder for hackers to crack. When someone knows your user name and password they have access to everything on your computer.

Journalist Chenda Ngak (2012) sited a report by SplashData, Inc. in an article about the 25 most common passwords.[7] According to password management company SplashData, the top three passwords of the year for 2012 were "password," "123456," and "12345678." The list of the 25 worst passwords of the year for 2012 was compiled by SplashData using information hackers posted in online forums and were said to be stolen passwords.

Ngak's article is an excellent short read and provides a few best practice recommendations everyone should consider when choosing a password. I suspect a similar study, if conducted several years later, would still find users choosing to use passwords that provide little to no protection.

OS Updates. You should always have your computer configured to automatically download and install and/or prompt you to download and install security patches.[8],[9],[10] These will help protect your computer from being compromised by threats (malware) that target known vulnerabilities. Security patches are issued to fix these problems. This is an essential step in your overall security that should be set up when you either install a new OS or when you set up a new computer.

If you choose not to set up automatic updates, then you should be disciplined enough to check for and install critical security updates on a routine basis. I recommend you check at least once a week if you choose not to use automatic updates.

Disable Unnecessary Services. This may seem like a daunting task because it sounds very technical, but it is one other step we can take to improve our overall security that may also result in improved system performance. All operating systems have services that run by default, so do not let operating specific examples used here influence your decision to spend a little time learning about this aspect of your OS.[11], [12], [13]

It doesn't matter if you're using a Mac, Linux, or Windows OS. Each may have unnecessary services running on your system with the potential of being exploited and compromising your system. Knowing which service to turn off and which to leave on may take a bit of research but it can result in improved security and performance.

From a security standpoint, it's a good idea to make your OS more secure by closing potential doors (services, in this case) a hacker or automated malware might use to compromise your system. From a performance standpoint, it's a good idea to turn off services your OS doesn't need, which may bog your system down, because it frees up RAM and CPU resources.

The services running on each OS are different, which is why you need to research the services running on your system to see if they are needed for your situation. For example, I use an HP Pavillion D9000 laptop with a LightScribe capable CD/DVD R/W drive with Microsoft Windows Vista. There is a LightScribe service that runs on startup automatically to make it always available. It may not use a lot of resources, but it is not necessary unless I'm going to use the LightScribe features to burn an image on a LightScribe compatible CD/DVD disk.

Another example is services for Bluetooth®. If it is available on your computer and you are not using this feature, then it's a good idea to disable it.

If you disable a service and then find something is not working you can simply start the service again. The bottom line – fewer unnecessary services running in the background can result in a smaller footprint (attack vector), more available RAM, and more CPU resources available for other services.

Firmware/BIOS Passwords

Each computer architecture used today provides a method to control the hardware features specific to your computer, such as boot sequence, video chip-set options, RAM configuration, etc., that are not specifically related to the operating system.

These technologies give you the option of requiring a password before your computer will boot the OS. This will allow you to provide another layer of protection for your computers that are physically protected from unauthorized access and slow down an attacker that gains unauthorized access. This should keep an average user from gaining access to your OS login prompt or from being able to boot your computer from any external media (portable hard drive, CD/DVD, or USB memory device). A skilled attacker can reset these passwords if they have physical access to your computer and be able to access your computer's login prompt or boot your computer using external media. This is also one of the reasons you should require passwords for your login prompt and encrypt your home directory or sensitive/private data.

A word of caution for some Mac users and raves for Apple.[14] The security of your portable Mac has gotten a lot better since 2011 when Apple changed how the firmware password is stored and reset in OS X for some laptops and portable devices (Mac mini, MacBook Air, MacBook Pro & iMac). Prior to this change, you could easily reset the firmware password by adding or removing hardware such as RAM. If you are using a Mac Desktop, then you should be able to reset the EFI password by following the directions in your version of Mac OS X Security Configuration Guide. Please see the references at the end of this chapter for links to Mac OS X Security Configuration guides.[15]

The UEFI specification also implements a process called Secure Boot that is intended to help protect your system from loading drivers or OS loaders that are not signed with a recognized digital signature.[16] According to Jake Edge, "secure boot" uses a digital signature database to help ensure only recognized and approved drivers and OS loaders are allowed to be processed. Any digital signatures that have been revoked or are not recognized would not be allowed to load in an effort to protect the system from malware.[17] You should consult your computer's documentation for more information on enabling or disabling any features in your BIOS, UEFI, or EFI.

Encrypt Home Directories/Folders

I cannot emphasize enough how important encryption is for your overall security. This is one of the most important best practices you can use to protect your sensitive data. You may not need to use it for your music or video, but you should consider it for your documents, spreadsheets, etc., that may contain sensitive information such as your SSN, tax information, banking account information, and a whole host of other information a hacker or cyber-criminal would love to get their hands on.

If you are a Mac or Linux user then you already have the ability to encrypt your home directories. If you are using any of the Microsoft Windows Home versions of operating systems then you do not have the ability of encrypting your data using the OS and will need additional software. Only Microsoft Windows XP/Vista/7/8 Professional, Business, or Enterprise versions give you the ability to encrypt folders or directories using built in encryption.

We've devoted a complete chapter to encryption because it is so important to your overall security. Take the time to learn about using encryption. It's not as difficult as it sounds at first and can mean the difference between a hacker or cyber-criminal getting access to your sensitive data or them coming up empty handed. You will rest a lot easier at night if your computer is stolen when your data is protected with encryption.

Power Down

If you are not using your computer then powering down is one of the best ways to protect your information. If it is not connected to the Internet and is powered down then hackers or malware cannot cause you harm. This is probably one of the simplest steps you can take to minimize your risks.

Summary

Get to know the features of your OS that can affect your security and take a little more control over your environment. It's not that difficult to implement most of the recommendations in this chapter and they will help you improve your security. There are a lot of resources on the Internet you can refer to which may provide more information to help you harden your OS.

See the references at the end of this chapter to learn more. Keep in mind that links are often changed or updated. We make no guarantee, implied or otherwise, as to the usefulness of any links referenced.

References

[1] Security Network and Attack Center (SNAC). Best Practices for Keeping Your Home Network Secure. http://www.nsa.gov/ia/_files/factsheets/Best_Practices_Datasheets.pdf

[2] Microsoft. Windows Vista Editions Compared. http://windows.microsoft.com/en-us/windows-vista/windows-vista-editions-compared-feature-by-feature-from-windows-vista-inside-out

[3] Wikipedia contributors. Windows 7 editions. Wikipedia, The Free Encyclopedia, http://en.wikipedia.org/w/index.php?title=Windows_7_editions&oldid=560965084

[4] Guy Thomas. Windows 8's Local Security Policy Editor. http://www.tomsitpro.com/articles/windows_8-secpol-local_security_policy_editor-group_policy,2-231.html

[5] Schroder, Carla. 2014. "How to Install and Try Linux the Absolutely Easiest and Safest Way | Linux.com." *Linux.com | The Source for Linux Information*. http://www.linux.com/learn/tutorials/770346-how-to-install-and-try-linux-the-absolutely-easiest-and-safest-way.

[6] "Cross-Site Scripting (XSS) - OWASP." 2014. *OWASP*. https://www.owasp.org/index.php/Cross-site_Scripting_(XSS).

[7] Chenda Ngak. CBS News. October 24, 2012. The 25 most common passwords of 2012. http://www.cbsnews.com/8301-205_162-57539366/the-25-most-common-passwords-of-2012/

[8] Windows Update. Microsoft. http://windows.microsoft.com/en-us/windows/help/windows-update

[9] Apple Inc. OS X: Updating OS X and Mac App Store apps. http://support.apple.com/kb/ht1338

[10] Linux-Security.net. Security Patches and Updates. http://www.linux-sec.net/Patches/

[11] Microsoft. Disable Unnecessary Services. http://msdn.microsoft. com/en-US/library/ms912889%28v=winembedded.5%29.aspx

[12] Ryan Faas. Computer World. Fifteen easy fixes for Mac security risks. http://www.macworld.com/article/1140268/macsecurityfixes.html?page=0

[13] University of California. Donald Bren School of Information and Computer Sciences. Unneeded Linux Services. http://www.ics.uci.edu/ computing/linux/services.php

[14] Topher Kessler. EFI firmware protection locks down newer Macs. http://reviews.cnet.com/8301-13727_7-57542601-263/efi-firmware-protection-locks-down-newer-macs/

[15] Apple Inc. Mac OS X Security Configuration Guides. https://ssl. apple.com/support/security/guides/

[16] Unified EFI, Inc. Unified Extensible Firmware Interface Specification. http://www.uefi.org/specs/download/UEFI_2_3_1_Errata_C_final

[17] Jake Edge. UEFI and "secure boot". http://lwn.net/Articles/447381/.

CHAPTER SIX

ENCRYPTION

_____

Encryption is often bypassed by many home users because it sounds like something that is too difficult to implement, or because they believe nothing they have on their computer or smart phone is really that important. They assume no one would be interested in their information because they believe it would not be of interest to someone else.

I cannot emphasize enough how wrong they are on both counts, today's encryption technologies are not difficult to understand or implement. There are a lot of identity thieves who appreciate people who believe their information is not important and don't do anything, or only do the bare minimum to protect themselves and their information.

There are a lot of options for anyone interested in learning more. Some of the solutions are so easy to use most people can begin using them with just a few clicks and have strong encryption protecting their data and privacy. The choices range from encrypting the entire computer's operating system/drive to encrypting only a folder or the home directory of the user. You might also encrypt a USB memory card or similar solid state memory device, or you may even encrypt your cloud storage such as Google Drive, Dropbox, SkyDrive, or box.

Other options include password protecting or encrypting only a file, encrypting each keystroke entered in a web browser or office application to avoid keyloggers, or using public key infrastructure (PKI) to encrypt email to and from other trusted users.

This chapter will introduce you to some of the software and tools available to everyone without needing to spend any extra money or buy anything extra. Many of these products can be used on multiple operating systems, which makes them ideal for home users and gives you a lot of options. These products can be used independently or in combination, so you can start with one product and add others as you become comfortable with them.

Keylogger Protection

You may be wondering what exactly is a keylogger and why would I need to worry about one? Keyloggers are programs that can be used for both legitimate and illegitimate purposes [1]. They allow the person who installed the program to record everything any user types on the computer's keyboard. Some businesses use keyloggers to help protect their intellectual property or to monitor employee activity. Keyloggers may also be used by law enforcement agencies during an investigation, or by parents who want to monitor what their children are doing when they are not around.

For our purposes, though, we'll assume you want to protect yourself from a keylogger that's installed without your knowledge for illegitimate purposes such as capturing your user name and password when you log into your bank, shopping online, social media network, or logging into your encrypted cloud drive.

You can now see how keyloggers can completely circumvent the security you use. The great news here is there are a number of different programs you can use which will help protect you from keyloggers if they happen to be installed on your computer. Obviously the best protection is to ensure they never get installed on your computer in the first place.

There are also other types of software that can be used to steal your information. These include:

- screen capture software that will take pictures of your desktop in an effort to collect information;

- clipboard capturing software to record anything you save to your clipboard;

- video capturing software that can activate your laptop or

smartphone camera and allow the person(s) using the software to watch you without your knowledge. You can place a piece of tape over the camera and microphone to mitigate this risk;

- audio capturing software that will turn on your microphone and allow them to hear anything you or others say within range of the microphone.

To protect against keyloggers you need to remember layers of security are better than just relying on one thing for your security. There are many different keyloggers out there and many traditional anti-virus/anti-malware software will not detect keyloggers or their variants.

Fortunately there are programs that will encrypt each and every keystroke you type to keep keyloggers from getting useful information. The anti-keylogger software does not keep the keylogger from capturing information. It encrypts everything you type so the keylogger doesn't get anything of value. See appendix one table 5 for some of the different packages currently available.

As with any software, you should read about the different features and choose the one that best meets your needs. My personal favorite is "KeyScrambler Personal" because it will achieve most of what I want when I'm using the Internet. If you want or need additional features you should consider purchasing one of the other packages, such as KeyScrambler Pro or GuardedID.

Whole Disk/Folder/File/Cloud Encryption

The software in this category probably makes many home users nervous at first because it requires a bit more time to set up and can be a little confusing. [2], [3],[4] Like most of the software we've covered so far, and will discuss in later chapters, some will be easy and some will require you to take your time, read, and understand both the technology and how it's used.

It's not necessary for you to learn about encryption algorithms to use the software in this category because the default or recommended settings are going to get you up and running with excellent protection out of the box. There are also a lot of good tutorials available on YouTube that will help you get started. See Appendix two for links to many of these tutorials.

One of the first questions you may ask is when would I want to use full disk encryption, folder encryption, file encryption, or cloud encryption? If you were a business executive and had to decide on the right solution or course of action for your situation, you might have someone develop a cost benefit analysis or risk analysis for each option. As a home user you can do the same thing without needing to consider everything a business executive might be faced with by asking yourself a few questions.

- What type of device am I using where I want to use encryption? Laptop, netbook, tablet, smart phone, desktop, or server?

- What type of information do I want to protect? Passwords, personal identifiable information (SSNs, date of birth, address, etc.), tax records, account information, etc.?

Once you've answered these simple questions, you can decide how best to use encryption. Consider the following scenarios:

- If you want to protect a mobile device, you might want to use full disk encryption to ensure if your device is stolen then your data is protected. If you also back up your data on a routine basis to an external device or to the cloud, then the only thing you've lost is the device.

- If you have a lot of sensitive information (SSNs, date of birth, address, etc.), tax records, account information, etc. on a desktop computer, you may only need to encrypt your folders.

- If you only have a few sensitive documents, you may decide to encrypt individual files.

- If you have a lot of sensitive information you need to have access to from anywhere, then storing it in the cloud with encryption is a great way to accomplish this. With cloud encryption, you've got some of the same options as you have on a local device. You can encrypt everything on your cloud drive/volume, or individual folders and files.

- If you are not comfortable using encryption in the cloud then you might want to use encryption on a removable device such as a USB hard drive or other solid state memory.

I want you to be aware that each situation may call for different software. See Appendix one, table four, for some of the different software packages you can use. Some of the software can be used for all the scenarios listed above, while others can only be used on the individual device. Some are more suited for or intended only for use with cloud computing.

When using encryption, you will use either a password, PIN, or token to enable encryption. You need to make sure you use best practices and choose a good password, lengthy PIN, or combination if using a token such as a YubiKey.

Here are some key points about passwords. Make them memorable, complex, and unique for each purpose rather than using the same password for every application. If you don't protect your data with a good password, then there really isn't much of a reason to use encryption. See chapter seven for a more detailed discussion on passwords.

File Level Password Protection

Many word processors today will allow you to password protect individual documents when you save them. Some give you the option of using passwords to protect them from being modified or to keep them from being opened without using a password. These options may or may not include encrypting the document, but they do help protect the file.

If you are using a word processor that does not have this option you may want to consider downloading LibreOffice or OpenOffice. Both productivity packages have versions for Windows, MAC OSX, and Linux. They're excellent products, and best of all, they're free. Alternatively you can choose one of the products listed in Appendix one, table four, that will allow you to encrypt individual files, folders, or drives.

References

[1] Dennis Fisher. 2013. "What Is a Keylogger?" Commercial. *Daily - English - Global - Blog.kaspersky.com*. http://blog.kaspersky.com/key-logger/.

[2] Disk encryption, http://en.wikipedia.org/w/index.php?title=Disk_encryption&oldid=607509275

[3] Filesystem-level encryption, http://en.wikipedia.org/w/index.php?title=Filesystem-level_encryption&oldid=583763552

[4] Cloud encryption, http://searchcloudstorage.techtarget.com/definition/cloud-storage-encryption

Chapter Seven

The Challenge of Passwords

Passwords, passwords, passwords. No one loves them, few really understand why we need them, and many people use the easiest password they can come up with when required because they have not been trained how to create a good password or, for that matter, why it's important.

In many cases, they will use a password such as a child or spouse's name, a favorite sports team, favorite automobile, or something related to their career. They may add a few numbers such as a birthday or another significant date, because they don't want to forget it, to make the password meet the complexity requirements of the account they are accessing.

If they have a hard time remembering the password, they will write it down on a note and hide it under their keyboard, in their day planner, store it in their phone, place it in their wallet, or just jot it down on a sticky note and leave it attached to their monitor. Worse yet, they may use the same user ID and password for many different accounts. If a hacker gets access to one account, then any other account using the same user ID and password should be considered compromised as well.

Hopefully you don't use any of the 25 most common passwords as reported by Chenda Ngak for CBS News in October of 2012.[1] The list included "password, 123456, abc123, monkey, iloveyou, football, jesus, and password1, to name a few.

Passwords like these can be guessed easily or broken by a hacker using a password cracking tool such as John the Ripper (Open Source), or L0phtCrack and the Password Recovery Toolkit (PRTK), which are commercial products. Some of these tools can

75

even be used to crack passwords written in 25 different languages, using combinations of special characters and numbers. All they need is time and patience. If you rarely change your passwords then they probably will have all the time they need to determine your password.

Password crackers are not the only tools a hacker or cybercriminal will use to collect passwords and account information. They may use social engineering to get unsuspecting users to disclose their password or have them click on a link in a craftily created email to reset their password.[2]

They may look over your shoulder while you type your password or install a keylogger that captures your user ID and passwords as you type. Keyloggers can be software or hardware, and if one is installed on your computer, then they have access to everything you type. In the case of a keylogger it does not matter how many times you change your password because they record everything you type.

Cyber criminals and hackers have a lot of motivation to harvest user IDs and passwords for profit, ranging from identity theft to banking fraud and account hijacking. If you are from or your banking accounts are in the United States, Canada, or Europe you have some protection from banking fraud, but nonetheless everyone collectively pays for banking fraud loss.[3]

Identity theft and account hijacking, however, can be a bit more challenging to recover from. For an example of a harrowing experience with account hijacking you should read James Fallows' article "Hacked!" documenting his wife's experience of having her Gmail account hacked.[4]

Remember, good security is not something you can set up once and forget. Good security does not consist of anti-virus protection alone. Good security is applied in layers and it takes an ongoing proactive, rather than a reactive, approach to achieve a measure of protection.

It would be nice if we could achieve good security simply by adding a new lock to our front door, but the days of single layer security are long since gone. Unless you live in a secluded location and do not use the Internet you should consider yourself vulnerable. Multiple layers of security provide the best protection and passwords are one of those layers.

It's always a good idea to develop good password habits to reduce the likelihood of becoming a victim of password theft that could result in bank fraud, identity theft, or account hijacking.

My purpose with this chapter is to help you understand the importance of good passwords and show you how to develop memorable and secure passwords. You can have the best security in the world, but if the password you use is easy to guess or crack then you may as well not waste your efforts to lock the door.

Complex passwords use a combination of upper and lower case characters, numbers, and special characters with a minimum length of eight characters. They can help you achieve a reasonable level of security and reduce your risk of compromise when you combine complex passwords with other layers of security, like changing your password often (at least once every few months, or sooner depending on the type of account).

Everyone should make an informed decision about the level of risk they are willing to take when it comes to passwords and security. The more you know about passwords and why they're important, the more likely you will choose to use good passwords.

Let's look at things you should do and things you should avoid when creating a password. I also want to show you a few tools you may consider when creating complex passwords so easy you only need to remember one good complex password, regardless of how many other accounts and passwords you have.

I want to encourage you to find a method of developing passwords that works best for you. One method may be easier for you than the other. I recommend you give each method a test drive and see which method helps you remember passwords without writing them down. I'll show you passwords created using mnemonics, altered passphrases, combining and altering words, and password derivations. I'll also share my personal favorite method, which is similar to password derivations.

Mnemonic Method

According to the Merriam-Webster online dictionary, mnemonics is a technique for improving memory.[6] In the case of passwords, it can definitely be used to help you create passwords that are easy to remember. All you need to do is take a phrase you already know and convert it to a password using the first letter of each word in the phrase to create your password. The more creative you are with this method the better your password will be.

Take a look at the examples below and you will understand how easy it can be to create good passwords using the mnemonic method.

Phrase	Password
One Nation under God indivisible with liberty and justice for all.	OnuGiwlajfa
One small step for man, one giant leap for mankind.	Ossfmoglfm
My grandmother always said, if you don't have anything good to say then don't say anything.	Mgasiydhagtstdsa

A word of caution with the use of mnemonics however; some password cracking software can be effective against mnemonic passwords through the use of custom dictionaries developed using commonly available phrases found on the Internet.[7] The best way to improve a mnemonic password that might be susceptible to this type of attack is to introduce variations that don't occur in the original phrase such as numbers, special characters (where allowed), and use upper and lower case letters. Or simply alter the phrase so it's different from the original.

Altered Passphrase

Altered passphrases will use mnemonics to create an initial pass phrase which will then be altered to introduce greater complexity but still be relatively easy to remember. An example of altering a pass phrase using the phrase "Mary had a little lamb whose fleece was white as snow" might be; Mh@1LwfWwa5.

It is a little difficult to see the difference at first, but there are upper and lower case characters along with one special character and two numbers. This particular example uses characters that resemble the letters that I would have used without introducing variations; mhallwfwwas.

The resulting password using the variations would be significantly more difficult for a hacker to crack yet will be relatively easy to remember. Take a look at the following examples using the phrases I used with the mnemonic only examples.

Phrase	Password
One Nation under God indivisible with liberty and justice for all.	On_Giw1aj4a
One small step for man, one giant leap for mankind.	Os54m1gLfm
My grandmother always said, if you don't have anything good to say then don't say anything.	Mg@5iydh@Gtstd5a

Combining and Altering Words

This is an interesting method that can create some very complex passwords and will allow you to use dictionary words for ease of remembering. The best way to do this is to choose two or three unrelated words and use upper case, lower case, special characters, and numbers to ensure the greatest complexity.

Unrelated words	Password
Grape cranes	Gr@peCr@ne5
Health green	H3@LthGrE3n
Dolphin rockets	D0lphinR*ck3t5

Password Derivations

This method was suggested by the National Institute of Standards and Technology (NIST) as an alternative to the previous three methods because of the difficulty people may have in remembering different passwords/passphrases for each different system or account they access.

With password derivations, you use a base password or passphrase that is altered slightly for each system you use. I found this method to be a bit more difficult to remember initially, but as with any password or passphrase, the more you use it the easier it will be for you to remember.

Base Password	System or Account	Resulting Password
Worldtravel	None	wOrlDtraVel
Prepend $6	System 1	$6wOrlDtraVel
Append $6	System 2	WOrlDtraVel$6
Insert $6 in the middle	System 3	wOrlD$6traVel

Significant Meaning

This is the method I have personally used for many years, very effectively. I do not claim to have developed this particular method, although no one taught me how to do this. It's similar to the altered password/passphrase method suggested by the NIST, but at the same time it is different enough that I wanted to share it here to give you another option.

This method has always allowed me to create a different password for each site I visit without needing to write the password down, and I've rarely had to request a password reset.

I choose a password based upon the website's name, the domain, or the subject of the website. By doing this you create a mental hook that will allow you to recall the base password the next time you visit.

I also use the same combination of altering upper case and lower case letters, numbers, and special characters in the same place for each password.

Base Password/Website/Domain	Password
Google	G2@o5&Ogle
Yahoo	Y2@a5&Hoo
Bing	B2@i5&Ng

When the system you are creating an account for has a minimum password length you can come up with another group of letters and numbers or special characters that you append to the beginning or end of the password.

An example using this method to get a password at least 14 characters long using the password above for Bing would be az7890B2@i5&Ng or B2@i5&Ngaz7890. If you continue to add the same characters to the beginning or end of your passwords to lengthen them when necessary you will easily remember your passwords, even when they are lengthy.

I recently read a blog post about passwords by Mauricio Estrella, which I'd recommend for everyone.[8] His method uses a similar construct to create passwords that have a significant meaning and allowed him to make positive changes in his life.

An example of a password using Mauricio's method might look like these examples:

Desired Change/Purpose	Password
Loose weight	E@tL3$$f00D
Complete a college degree	1m0r3cL@s$
Save for a new car	G3t@newChevy$$

Password Management Software

You may be thinking to yourself, why would I need a password manager? Well, if you only have a few accounts you may not need a password manager, but research indicates many people will use the same user ID and password for multiple accounts.[9]

According to the same research, most users have more than six passwords that are shared on three or more sites. Considering they may have upwards of 25 different accounts that require passwords, the average user will need to enter approximately 8 passwords per day. You may not fit into this profile, but if you do then you really should consider a password management tool.

There are some excellent password management packages with a lot of different features regardless of your platform of choice (Windows, MAC, Linux). The most important feature I looked for in a password management package is encryption. I want to make sure my passwords are stored securely, whether they are stored on my computer, on a removable media drive, or in the cloud. There are a lot of other great features such as auto-login, one time passwords, two-factor authentication, and more.

Password management software requires a master password, or in some cases a master password and token of some kind, to provide greater security that is used to access your stored passwords. These systems allow you to have a complex password for each and every account you use without needing to remember the user ID or the password.

This also makes using and remembering a lot of different passwords a thing of the past. Some of these tools will also automatically detect when you are creating an account or changing your password and will generate a suggested password. Two of the programs I reviewed for this chapter will also automatically enter your user ID and password when you log into different accounts.

When I first shared these tools with my friends and family, I had a good friend who pointed out the fact that if someone gains access to the master password they would have access to all the accounts these protect. This is definitely a true statement which is why it's very important you understand the need for creating and using complex passwords and how to protect them.

Fortunately, there are other ways to make some of the current password management software even more secure using an inexpensive USB device that generates a one-time password each time you log into your password management software.[9]

YubiKey

When I started researching password management software, I ran across the YubiKey and immediately decided to get one because it provides an extra layer of security for your accounts by allowing you to set up two-factor authentication.

What is two-factor authentication and why would anyone want to use it? It's more than just a user ID and password. It requires something you have (YubiKey) and something you know (user ID and password).

Everything I teach about security emphasizes security in depth or layers of security, and using something like a YubiKey is a good way of enhancing your security.

The YubiKey allows you to add another layer of security to your password management. Even if a hacker learns your master password they cannot gain access to your passwords unless they have your YubiKey.

At the time of this writing, the YubiKey allows you to add two-factor authentication to six different password managers. The YubiKey is a unique USB device that is platform independent and cannot be duplicated or copied. Each YubiKey is different and generates a new one time password (OTP) each time you use it that is nearly impossible to spoof.[10]

Summary

Passwords are a very important layer of security you can implement using different strategies to improve your overall security. A good password is one that is at least eight characters long (the longer the better), uses upper case and lower case characters, numbers, special characters, and is changed on a routine basis.

Password managers can help you create complex passwords for all of your accounts and store them securely using encryption. When using a password manager, you should ensure your master password is a very good complex password because it is used to protect all of your passwords. You can use a YubiKey or similar device to add another layer of security to your password manager by allowing you to set up two-factor authentication.

References

[1] C. Ngak. The 25 most common passwords of 2012. http://www.cbsnews.com/8301-205_162-57539366/the-25-most-common-passwords-of-2012/

[2] Sara Granger. Social Engineering Fundamentals, Part I: Hacker Tactics. http://www.symantec.com/connect/articles/social-engineering-fundamentals-part-i-hacker-tactics

[3] Dinei Florêncio and Cormac Herley. Is Everything We Know About Password Stealing Wrong? http://research.microsoft.com/pubs/161829/EverythingWeKnow.pdf

[4] James Fallows. Hacked! http://www.theatlantic.com/magazine/archive/2011/11/hacked/308673/

[5] Karen Scarfone and Murugiah Souppaya. NIST SP 800-118 "Guide to Enterprise Password Management". http://csrc.nist.gov/publications/drafts/800-118/draft-sp800-118.pdf

[6] Merriam-Webster. Mnemonics. http://www.merriam-webster.com/dictionary/mnemonics

[7] Cynthia Kuo, Sasha Romanosky, Lorrie Faith Cranor. Human Selection of Mnemonic Phrase-based Passwords. http://repository.cmu.edu/cgi/viewcontent.cgi?article=1043&context=isr

[8] Mauricio Estrella. 2014. "How a Password Changed My Life | Mauricio Estrella." http://www.huffingtonpost.com/mauricio-estrella/how-a-password-changed-my-life_b_5567161.html.

[9] Dinei Florêncio and Cormac Herley. A Large-Scale Study of Web Password Habits. https://research.microsoft.com/pubs/74164/www2007.pdf

[10] Yubico. Technical description. How the YubiKey Standard works. http://www.yubico.com/products/yubikey-hardware/yubikey/technical-description/

CHAPTER EIGHT

WEB BROWSER SECURITY

Security When Browsing

This is probably one of the most important chapters where you can apply specific measures to improve your security. Just about everything you do on the Internet requires a web browser, so hardening your browser settings is important.

Most web browsers are not configured for the best security out of the box, which can result in a lot of problems if you don't tighten it up a bit. If you visit a website that has been compromised with malware and haven't changed the default settings on your computer then your system is more vulnerable. You may wind up with malware installed without your knowledge but tightening up your settings can help prevent this vulnerability.

There are a lot of factors that can affect this, but it's a good idea to take a little time to configure your browser with a bit more security than the default configuration and, in some cases, install an add-on application to enhance the security features of your browser.

One thing is for certain. Cyber criminals are constantly trying to find vulnerabilities in popular browsers and browser extensions in order to exploit them for financial gain. I'm not talking about someone who is hacking for fun, but criminals whose sole motivation for doing what they do each day is to find a way of taking other people's money. I want to help you do everything you can to improve your overall security.

Good security is applied in layers. I know I've said this many times throughout this book, however, I learned long ago the secret to understanding and application is repetition. The more you hear someone emphasize something the more likely you are to listen and apply what you learn.

Updates

Just like your operating system, and any other software for that matter, it's critical for good security to ensure your web browser is kept up to date. Most of today's browsers will alert you when an update is available and in some cases you can configure your browser to automatically download and install the updates. How easy is that?

If you do not have automatic updates configured then when a new release is available you should download it and start using the new release. Don't allow criminals to take advantage of your system because you are running an older browser that can be attacked using a known vulnerability.

Settings

Browsers are providing better security by default, but there are still a lot of optional settings you should understand. Web browser developers have to walk a fine line between making their products fast, full featured, and secure, but in order to do so they may dial back some of the security features that reduce performance.

This helps developers attract users because everyone wants a fast, full featured web browser that is secure. However, default settings are often less secure in order to achieve better performance. Most of the information in this chapter will be related to steps you can take to improve security regardless of the browser or operating system you are using.[1] There will also be a few important tips related to specific browsers and operating systems.

Passwords

By now you have already read about passwords and password management tools; if you have not, then I want to encourage you to review chapter seven. Almost all browsers have a built-in password manager. I recommend you do not use the built-in password managers. Instead, you should begin using a good password management tool that allows you to encrypt your passwords with the best publicly available encryption, will automatically generate complex passwords, and will auto-fill and auto-login for you.

The last two features are personal preference because, like most people, I enjoy added features that enhance my overall experience. I recommend you find a password manager that is platform independent so it will work with Windows, Linux, or Mac, as well as most smart phones.

Again, if you haven't read the section on passwords and password management software I want to encourage you to take some time and consider your options.

If you are a Windows user and decide to use a built-in password manager, then your best options are Firefox or Safari because they will encrypt your passwords if you use a master password. Keep in mind however, if you do not use a master password then your passwords are not encrypted and anyone with physical access to your computer will be able to copy your user IDs and passwords.

If your passwords are not encrypted, then it is also possible for malware on a compromised or malicious website to download or copy your built-in password manager by exploiting a vulnerability in your browser. Keeping your browser updated with security patches or by installing the latest version of your favorite browser will reduce your risks and vulnerabilities.

The Safari browser has versions for both Mac and Windows users. Both Firefox and Safari offer basic encryption of userid and passwords.

Firefox and Safari use Triple DES encryption for password management when you use a master password. It is acceptable encryption if you are using complex passwords and do not share passwords across multiple sites.[2],[3]

Neither Internet Explorer (through version 10) or Google Chrome have a built-in password manager. Internet Explorer is a little more secure than a few of the other browsers because it does not have a show password option for stored passwords. Google Chrome does allow you to set a master password if you choose to snyc your Gmail account, but this shouldn't be confused with a password manager.[4]

If you are a MAC user, then you are probably already familiar with Keychain.[5] Keychain has been around since MAC OS 8.6. If you are using a new MAC, then you have access to an excellent password manager. It is also available as iCloud Keychain for iPhone, iPad, and iPod running iOS 7.0.3 or later and MAC OSX v10.9 and later. The iCloud version of Keychain uses stronger encryption, but regardless of the version you are using your passwords will be secure.

Enable Phishing and Malware Protection

Each browser uses a slightly different technology to help block known malicious websites. Chrome, Firefox, and Safari use Google's Safe Browsing Application Programming Interface (API).[6] Google's Safe Browsing is a service that allows these browsers to use the service to automatically check URLs against Google's database of known or suspected phishing and malware pages.

Browsers that only use Google's Safe Browsing API do not have the same level of protection as Google's Chrome browser. This is because Google has included additional protection within the Chrome browser to defend against drive-by malware downloads.

Internet Explorer, on the other hand, uses its SmartScreen Filter, which works in much the same way as Google's Safe Browsing API service. The SmartScreen Filter also checks files downloaded from the Internet against a dynamically changing list of known malicious software.

NSS Labs is an information security research company that researches web browsers annually against known malware using scenarios to emulate typical user behavior. This research is available for anyone in an easy-to-read research paper. Their findings for 2013 were interesting to say the least. The following are excerpts from the NSS Labs report.

Five leading browsers were tested against 754 samples of real world malicious software. Major differences in the ability to block malware were observed. Data represented in this report was captured over 28 days through NSS Labs' unique live testing harness. The data provides insight into the built-in protection capabilities of modern browsers, including Chrome, Firefox, Internet Explorer, Opera, and Safari.

For every 10 web encounters with socially engineered malware, Firefox and Safari users will be protected from approximately one attack. This implies that 9 out of 10 browser malware encounters will test the defenses of installed anti-virus or other operating system defenses. Chrome users will be protected from just over 8 out of 10 attacks, and Internet Explorer 10 users will generally be afforded protection from all but 4 out of 1000 socially engineered malware attacks. It should be noted that some of the download protection mechanisms require a user choice, and this can decrease the effectiveness of the protections. Opera users are afforded virtually no protection against socially engineered malware.

I encourage you to download and read the NSS report as well as any others on their site.[6] The more you read, the more you will understand even technically challenging security topics.

Disable JAVA Plug-ins

JAVA is a development language used to build applications on many different systems. It is used extensively with online gaming websites, banking websites that provide loan calculators, and even with chat applications, just to name a few.[7]

JAVA is also OS independent, meaning you may be vulnerable to JAVA exploits whether you are using a MAC, Linux, Windows, or other mobile device that uses JAVA. There are millions of users on the Internet who have JAVA installed which makes it a prime target for exploitation by cyber criminals.

While it is one of the most targeted applications on the Internet, you can still take steps to improve your security because it is not required for you to browse the Internet.

When JAVA is enabled, your computer can be exploited if you visit a website that has been compromised by hackers or cyber criminals. There are many steps you can take to mitigate or reduce this kind of threat, such as:

- Keep your version of JAVA up to date. Enable automatic downloading or download updates manually so you are protected from known vulnerabilities.

- Disable JAVA in your browser using the JAVA control panel. JAVA provides detailed security configuration documentation that is easy for anyone to apply. You don't need to be a computer guru, so head over to www.java.com and search on "security". This will give you access to easy-to-follow steps for securing JAVA on your specific platform/operating system.

- Do not surf the Internet as a privileged user with JAVA enabled.

- Use your browser's built-in reputation filter or try the "Web of Trust" plug-in for your browser to help protect you from known malicious websites.

- Heed the warnings of your browser and make sure you understand the warning before you ignore it.

- Setup OpenDNS or Norton ConnectSafe for Home, which can enhance your browsing by adding an additional layer of security.

Brian Krebs, who runs the KrebsonSecurity, made an excellent recommendation.[7] If you disable the JAVA plug-in in your browsers but need to enable JAVA on a specific website or websites, then a good option is to configure a different browser you use only for accessing those sites.

This will allow you to keep tighter security on the browser you use for most of your Internet browsing.

JavaScript

I want to make sure you understand there is a difference between

JAVA and JavaScript. They are similar in name but have completely different uses. JavaScript is a scripting language used on many websites to provide you the interactive environment we have all come to expect when we visit a website. JAVA is a programming language used to develop applications, some of which may run through a website, but JAVA and JavaScript are two distinct tools used by developers.

JavaScript can also be used to serve up malware to the unprotected browser/OS. The problem with JavaScript is there isn't an easy way to fully protect yourself because it's so widely used. So what can you do to enhance your security if you cannot fully protect yourself?

MAC OS X: I'm not personally a fan of MAC computers, but I've got to give raves to Apple in this case. I could not find a lot of warnings about MAC OS X or the Safari browser. Safari provides you a sandbox environment designed to protect your system from malware by restricting what websites can do. Basically, the sandbox feature keeps anything downloaded inside the sandbox, and it is automatically deleted when your session is over. Safari also runs each web page in a different process so any harmful code would not be able to affect your whole browser.[8] We'll talk more about ways to run all your browsers in a sandbox in another section to really step up your browsing security.

Internet Explorer: You can disable scripts in Internet Explorer completely, enable it for all, or have Internet Explorer prompt you. The problem with the last option is you'll be responding to a never-ending stream of prompts. Obviously, if you enable it for all, you are not protected at all; if you disable it for all, then many website features will not work.

Firefox: Firefox has a lot of add-ons that can enhance your security, and many of them are free. NoScript is one such add-on for Firefox by Giorgio Maone. According to Giorgio, NoScript is a whitelist-based security tool which disables all the executable web content (JavaScript and Java by default, but also Flash and other plugins on demand) and lets the user choose on the fly, with a single click, the "trusted sites" where these potentially dangerous technologies are allowed.[9]

I have used NoScript, and it works as advertised. You do need a little patience because you need to make a choice each time you visit a new website. I don't know too many users, myself included, who only visit specific sites. The Internet is too large, and we are too curious for our own good sometimes.

Chrome: Chrome has a built in feature for handling scripting that is similar to NoScript but with fewer options. When you disable scripting in Chrome and visit a website that has JavaScript, there will be a red "X" in the address bar. When you click on the red "X", you are given the option to enable scripting for this website or leave it disabled.

One of the main differences in the way this feature works in Chrome and the NoScript add-on for Firefox is there is no option to disable third-party JavaScript content. Your only option is to either enable JavaScript or disable JavaScript.

Fortunately, there is also an add-on similar to NoScript for the Chrome browser called NotScripts. In fact, according to Eric Wong who authored the Google Chrome add-on, NotScripts was inspired by NoScript. NotScripts will allow you to block third-party JavaScript content and provides much of the same functionality as NoScript.[10]

One thing is for sure, if you choose to use either Firefox or Google Chrome with one of the available script blocking add-ons such as NoScript or NotScripts, it will take some time to get set up properly. According to Brian Krebs, "selectively script blocking can take some getting used to. Most script-blocking add-ons will disable scripting by default on Web sites that you have not added to your trusted list. In some cases, it may take multiple tries to get a site that makes heavy use of JavaScript to load properly."[7]

ActiveX Filtering

According to Microsoft, ActiveX controls are small programs that are also known as add-ons used on the Internet to enhance user experiences.[11] If you are not using Internet Explorer, then you are not likely to be vulnerable to any ActiveX vulnerability. This is because ActiveX controls are not supported by other browsers. I recommend you steer clear of any plug-ins for other browsers that claim to support ActiveX.

If you have a website that requires ActiveX controls for a specific application you need or want to run, then you will need to use Internet Explorer for that website. The website should prompt you to download the required ActiveX control and inform you what the control is required for.

Fortunately, Internet Explorer is designed to block websites from using an ActiveX control if it detects the control being used in a way that seems unsafe. You should also delete any unneeded ActiveX controls you have downloaded. The steps are pretty easy:

- Select the "Tools" menu in Internet Explorer
- Select the "Manage add-ons" menu under the "Tools" menu
- Once the "Manage add-ons" interface is active, select "Toolbars and Extensions"
- Select the "Downloaded controls" in the drop-down menu listed below the "Tracking Protection" menu.
- Select the ActiveX control you want to delete.
- Select the "delete" button and you are done.

Internet Explorer also offers you the option of filtering ActiveX controls which are downloaded to your computer and will allow you to choose which websites you allow to run ActiveX controls.[12]

This is a very important feature because you may find after you download an ActiveX control for a specific website that other websites are also able to use the control.

Using the ActiveX filter will allow you to choose which websites can run ActiveX controls and will block websites that are not approved from running these controls. You can enable ActiveX filtering by using the following steps:

- Select the "Tools" menu in Internet Explorer
- Select the "ActiveX filtering" option under the "Tools" menu

This is all that's required to enable ActiveX filtering in Internet Explorer. Once it is enabled, you'll have a blue icon that looks like a circle with a line from the upper left to the lower right of the circle adjacent to your address bar. This blue icon indicates ActiveX controls are being filtered. Just click on the blue icon to disable ActiveX filtering on websites you choose to trust.

Cookies

How do you like your Oreo cookies? Cookies are often misunderstood. Let me reassure you that cookies cannot be used to run programs on your computer, nor can they be used to spread viruses.[13] They are not programs but are actually text files exchanged with each server you visit and stored in your browser.

Cookies are used to identify you as you navigate through the website (session) and to maintain your user preferences when you return to a website where you are able to modify your profile settings (persistent). There are also cookies described as third-party cookies because they provide content mostly in the form of advertisements from an outside server on the website you are visiting.

Persistent cookies, as the name implies, generally have a long life and are stored in your browser unless you delete them, whereas session cookies are only used for tracking your session through a website where you must be authenticated such as Amazon, your banking website, or Facebook.

A good example is when you are shopping on Amazon and put an item in your shopping cart. The session cookie allows Amazon to keep track of each item you put in the cart and have them available for you when you check out. Session cookies are not stored in your browser but are stored in memory so they do not have a long life.

The next thing you need to understand is that the first two cookies described above are very important. Third party cookies, however, are not important. While they do not necessarily pose a security threat to you, there are privacy concerns because these cookies can track your movements between websites when you visit other websites that have content from the same third-party.[14]

So, now that you know what a cookie is, you may want to modify how your browser handles third-party cookies and have it delete or not accept third-party cookies. See the links for each browser below to learn how to modify the latest browsers to delete third-party cookies.

Internet Explorer: http://windows.microsoft.com/en-us/internet-explorer/delete-manage-cookies#ie=ie-11

Mozilla Firefox: https://support.mozilla.org/en-US/kb/disable-third-party-cookies

Google Chrome: https://support.google.com/chrome/answer/114836?hl=en&ref_topic=3421433

Safari: Again I've got to rave about Apple because the Safari browser blocks third-party cookies by default. If you are using a MAC or other Apple product that uses the Safari browser, then you don't need to do anything.[15]

Mac Browser Security

Safari is the default web browser built into the Mac OS X platform. While Mac OS X seems to be focused on security out of the box, Apple still provides recommendations you can use to make your browsing a little more secure. For specifics, see the security configuration guides provided by Apple for each version of OS X.[16]

Quick Browser Checkup

Qualys BrowserCheck is a free online scanner that will check your computer's browser and verify if you have the latest version, check for out-of-date plug-ins, missing OS security patches, and even recommend changes to your browser's configuration to improve your security.[17]

The best thing about the Qualys BrowserCheck is that it works with Internet Explorer, Firefox, and Chrome on Windows. It works with Safari, Chrome, and Firefox on the Mac OS, and will even scan browsers in Linux systems to verify the current browser.

The BrowserCheck can be installed as a plug-in or it can scan your system without any additional software. Installing the plug-in gives you more features, so this is the recommended configuration. You can use the BrowserCheck by going to the following URL in order to quickly scan your computer: https://browsercheck.qualys. com/.

Sandboxing

The idea of running your browser in a sandbox was mentioned earlier in this chapter. There is no better time than now to start using this type of security when you consider how fast the threats have grown in the past few years. There really isn't a completely safe platform out there. Let's look at a few options you might use to provide you with a sandbox.

Sandboxie is a Windows-based program that is designed to allow you to run any application and therefore any browser in a sandbox.[18] It's almost like running a virtual machine that is completely separate from your files and operating system. Any malicious files or viruses that might be downloaded without your knowledge are contained in the sandbox.

You can allow JAVA apps, JavaScript, and ActiveX controls to run without worrying about infecting your system. When you close the program everything is deleted from memory, which keeps your system protected.

Home users can download Sandboxie and use it for free but after 30 days you'll be asked if you want to upgrade to the full version which sells for 15 Euros. The dollar price fluctuates depending on the exchange rate, but it's approximately $20, so this is an excellent deal.

There are also two Windows-based programs which provide

some sandbox functionality by monitoring your programs for malicious behavior. When they detect anything that seems malicious, they will automatically create a sandbox for the process. Comodo Internet Security has this feature in its free version, and Avast Premier 2014 includes a similar feature in its commercial version.[19],[20]

If I keep this up I'm going to have to purchase a Mac system because again I've got to rave about the Mac OS X. It's the first OS I've found that has a sandbox built in, the "App Sandbox".

According to Apple, App sandboxing isolates apps from the critical system components of your Mac, your data, and your other apps. Even if an app is compromised by malicious software, sandboxing automatically blocks it to keep your computer and your information safe.

OS X Mavericks delivers even better sandboxing protection in Safari by sandboxing the built-in PDF viewer and plug-ins such as Adobe Flash Player, Silverlight, QuickTime, and Oracle Java. And OS X Mavericks sandboxes apps like the Mac App Store, Messages, Calendar, Contacts, Dictionary, Font Book, Photo Booth, Quick Look Previews, Notes, Reminders, Game Center, Mail, and FaceTime."[21]

References

[1] Security Network and Attack Center (SNAC). Best Practices for Keeping Your Home Network Secure. http://www.nsa.gov/ia/_files/factsheets/Best_Practices_Datasheets.pdf

[2] Erik Kangas. Master Password Encryption in Firefox and Thunderbird. http://luxsci.com/blog/master-password-encryption-in-firefox-and-thunderbird.html

[3] Triple DES Validation List. National Institute of Standards and Technology. http://csrc.nist.gov/groups/STM/cavp/documents/des/tripledesval.html

[4] Melanie Pinola. Which Password Manager is the Most Secure? Lifehacker. http://lifehacker.com/5944969/which-password-manager-is-the-most-secure

[5] Christopher Breen. How to manage Passwords with Keychain.

Macworld. *http://www.macworld.com/article/2013756/how-to-manage-passwords-with-keychain-access.html*

[6] Abrams, R.; Pathak, J.; & Barrera, O. (2013) Browser Security Comparative Analysis: Socially Socially Engineered Malware Blocking. https://www.nsslabs.com/reports/2013-browser-security-comparative-analysis-socially-engineered-malware

[7] Brian Krebs. What you need to know about the JAVA exploit. KrebsonSecurity. http://krebsonsecurity.com/2013/01/what-you-need-to-know-about-the-java-exploit/

[8] Apple. Safari, browse the web in smarter, more powerful ways. https://www.apple.com/safari/

[9] Giorgio Maone. NoScript. http://maone.net/

[10] Eric Wong. NotScripts. http://optimalcycling.com/other-projects/notscripts/

[11] Microsoft. Protect yourself when you use ActiveX controls. Safety and Security Center. http://www.microsoft.com/security/pc-security/activex.aspx

[12] Microsoft. About ActiveX filtering. Safety and Security Center. http://ie.microsoft.com/testdrive/browser/activexfiltering/about.html

[13] Microsoft. Description of Cookies. http://support.microsoft.com/kb/260971

[14] A. Barth. HTTP State Management Mechanism. Internet Engineering Task Force (IETF). *http://tools.ietf.org/pdf/rfc6265.pdf*

[15] Apple. Safari – The smartest way to surf. https://www.apple.com/safari/

[16] Apple. Mac OS X Security Configuration Guides. https://www.apple.com/support/security/guides/

[17] Qualys. BrowserCheck. https://browsercheck.qualys.com/

[18] Sandboxie Holdings, LLC. Sandboxie. http://www.sandboxie.com/

[19] Comodo Group, Inc. Free Internet Security. http://www.comodo.com/home/internet-security/free-internet-security.php

[20] Avast Software Inc. avast! Premier 2014. http://www.avast.com/en-us/premier

[21] Apple. Sandboxing blocks malicious code. https://www.apple.com/osx/what-is/security.html

CHAPTER NINE

EMAIL SECURITY

Email may be a gaping hole in your overall security, or it may only be a mouse hole. It all depends on your personal email habits. If you are among the millions of users whose use of smart phones with texting and instant messaging has changed how you keep in contact with friends and family, you may not even use email much on your personal computer.

Regardless of how you now communicate, the principals outlined in this chapter can just as easily be applied to your use of texting and instant messaging and will help you stay safe when you do use email.

The goal of this chapter is to make you aware of the vulnerabilities related to using email that can result in your computer or smart phone/tablet being compromised. Hopefully you will learn some new things you may not have considered before.

We'll look at spam, phishing, unsolicited email (which may or may not be spam/phishing), public key infrastructure, dealing with attachments, and we'll also discuss the pros and cons of using email clients or web-based email.

The last section will look at some of the options you can configure in your mail client or web-based email accounts to improve your security.

SPAM

I'm assuming anyone reading this book already knows what SPAM is. I don't know of any way to completely eliminate SPAM from making it to your in-box. There are so many ways for SPAM to be propagated and for spammers to get your email address. They can do this even if you don't post messages using your email address in public forums or commercial websites that might sell your information.

The following tips are offered for your consideration and may help, but nothing will eliminate SPAM completely. [2]

Be protective of your email address. Only give your email address to people you trust. You may also want to ask your contacts not to send you an email that is being sent to a group of people unless they use the blind copy (Bcc:) function. If you have had an email address for a long time, then this tip will probably not be too helpful since it's very likely spammers already have your email address.

You might want to consider setting up a new email address and only share it with specific people, while checking your well known address periodically to ensure you receive email from others who only have your older address.

I don't recommend you get rid of or delete your older email address because many times you use your email address when creating an online account and the email address is used to reset your account's log-in information. If you changed your email address and needed to reset one of the accounts that used your old email address, you may have problems resetting the account.

You could also use the older email account when filling out forms. It has become common place for businesses, hospitals, public offices, schools, and a host of other organizations to ask for your email address on all sorts of forms.

While giving your email address out may seem harmless, you don't know what your information will be used for. It might be used to send you useful information such as coupons, information about specials, or it might be sold to others who will then start sending you SPAM. If you use two email addresses, you'll be able to segregate your email address for different purposes and keep one for communication with friends, family, and colleagues, with the other used when filling out forms, etc.

In spite of all these efforts, you may still fall victim to spammers if yours or a friend's computer falls victim to malware that hijacks your address book in order to send SPAM. In this case, everyone in the address book will likely start seeing the same SPAM.

Use a SPAM filter. You may or may not have a lot of options to use or not use a SPAM filter. If you are using one of the web-based email providers such as Yahoo mail, Google Mail, Hotmail, etc., then you already have a SPAM filter doing some work for you. If you are using a mail client like Outlook, Thunderbird, or Apple Mail, you should have a SPAM filter plug-in or add-on program running on your computer.

I read an interesting blog post by Ian "Gizmo" Richards who writes for the TechSupportAlert website.[3] He said the email address he uses for blogging receives close to 1000 SPAM emails daily. The time it took for his Outlook plug-in to process his email was beginning to take a long time until he started having his email forwarded to Gmail because they have an excellent SPAM filter. Doing that reduced the amount of SPAM he received to approximately 50 emails a day. He was able to do this because Gmail allows you to download your email using POP3. He then uses Cloudmark DesktopOne to filter the remaining 50 emails.

Gmail's filter processes all email automatically so only about five percent of the daily SPAM is downloaded when you access your GMail account using your mail client/POP3. The combination of the 2 filters working together ensures 99% of all SPAM is eliminated.

That is not necessarily impressive since there are other client-based SPAM filters that do this as well, but what is impressive with this configuration is that both the Gmail filter and the Cloudmark filter recognize 99% of all legitimate email, which means you almost never need to worry about missing an important email because it was detected as SPAM by your filter.

Best of all is the fact this configuration is free. Cloudmark has a premium version available for an annual subscription of $19.95, but the basic version will work for most situations.

Occasionally you will receive SPAM with attachments and even email from your contacts with attachments. If you are using a mail client, it is important to configure the mail client to allow you to pre-view the email without opening it to limit potential malware from causing problems.

You should delete all email with attachments you are not ex-pecting, and be cautious with attachments received from your con-tacts. Most anti-virus programs will scan attachments for malware/ viruses, which will help mitigate many threats. If your anti-virus program does not automatically scan email attachments you should save them in a separate folder and scan them before opening them.

You will still need to exercise some caution and decide if the risk is worth opening an attachment, even from your contacts, because new malware is proliferated daily across the Internet. This means at some point your anti-virus software is not going to recognize mal-ware and you may fall victim. If this happens and you are using the recommendations in this book, you should be able to recover with-out too much trouble.

Summary

This is a relatively short chapter because many of the problems you'll face with SPAM and email are addressed in other sections (malware, viruses, Trojans, etc). Exercise prudence with your email and think before you click.

If I suspect an email from a contact is not legitimate, I always send them an email asking if they sent the email. I do this because they may not be as security conscious as I am and may themselves be victims of malware that's sending email to everyone in their ad-dress book.

The more you become familiar with SPAM, the more likely you'll recognize when you've received email that is not legitimate. There are so many scams out there and variations on each piece of SPAM that is marginally successful because the cyber criminals behind them are making money. Become familiar with the telltale evidence of SPAM and you'll reduce your risks by taking the actions outlined here.

References

[1] History of email spam," Wikipedia, The Free Encyclopedia, http://en.wikipedia.org/w/index.php?title=History_of_email_spam&oldid=601820583

[2] "Reducing Spam | US-CERT." 2014. http://www.us-cert.gov/ncas/tips/ST04-007.

[3] How to reduce spam. TechSupportAlert. http://www.techsupportalert.com/how_to_reduce_spam.htm

Chapter Ten

Mobile Devices

Smart Phones and Tablets (Mobile Devices)

The first thing you need to understand up front is your smart phone or tablet is a computer. It may be small and may not work exactly like your desktop or laptop, but it is definitely a computer. I have many friends who have gigabytes of pictures, video, and even a good deal of personally identifying information on their smart phones.

When cell phones started becoming popular they were no different than your wireless home phone, except that you could take it with you everywhere. Then cell phone companies started including other applications to make your phone more useful.

Today's smart phones are more powerful than many of the computers we were using in the 80's and 90's. If you remember that your smart phone or tablet is actually a computer and not just a phone, then you are more likely to apply some or all of the sound security principals discussed in this and other chapters to make your mobile computing more secure. For the purpose of this chapter we'll refer to smart phones and tablets as mobile devices, unless there is a specific need to identify one over the other.

There are clear differences between the levels of risks one accepts by default when you use a mobile device. I'm not a personal fan of Apple's Mac iOS for a number of reasons, but I've got to admit they have a very secure platform and give credit where credit is due.[1]

Apple's iOS is virtually free of malware while the Android OS platform has seen phenomenal malware growth in the past few years. SophosLabs reported they've identified more than 650,000 individual pieces of malware and discover almost 2000 new malware daily.[2] Cisco also reported that 99% of all mobile malware discovered in 2013 targeted the Android platform.[3] With news like this I'm almost ready to embrace the Apple iPhone.

Operating System Updates

Let's get started now by applying some of the principals we've already discussed, such as ensuring automatic updates are enabled for your device. This may be a little more challenging than setting up automatic updates on your home computer because there are so many mobile device vendors who have different methods of delivering updates.

Does your service plan have limits on your data? If so, you may want to see if you can disable updates when you are not connected to a trusted Wi-Fi network. I find the best way to ensure my mobile devices are kept updated is to check for updates only when I'm on my home network. Check the vendor's website for your make/model to find the best way to keep your mobile device's OS updated and more secure. This way you are sure to have the most recent updates.

Physical Security

There is a growing trend of theft of mobile devices which is alarming. According to a Consumer Reports survey, there were 3.1 million smart phones stolen in 2013, and it's expected to grow to more than 4 million in 2014[4].

There are several things you can do to make your mobile device more secure, with physical security being the focus. Most of the security features that fall in this category are available on your mobile device regardless of OS.

Take a few minutes to learn about your mobile device's built in security settings so you can apply them from day one. If you are not using any of these recommendations then start using them to improve your security. We'll look at a PIN/password, encryption, storage strategies, and location services.

PINs/Passwords: Right up front you should setup a PIN or password and have it locked after a few minutes of inactivity. Take a few minutes and find your phone's security settings to enable a PIN lock on your phone to help protect your phone from the curious. It may not stop a thief who knows what they are doing from gaining access to your data, but it will keep less technical snoops from accessing your phone and data.

Encryption: This step is not much more difficult to setup than setting up a PIN/Password for your mobile device. We'll assume your mobile device's security settings also has an option for you to encrypt your drive. I have a Motorola Moto G and was able to set up encryption without much trouble. Setting up encryption will ensure that if anyone steals your mobile device then they will not have access to your personal data unless they also know your PIN.

Visual Observation: If you do set up either a PIN-only configuration or encryption, you will need to be aware of your surroundings. A lot of thieves are able to get into a mobile device because they are observant. They may record you entering your PIN for use at a later time or they may watch you enter your PIN once or over time and remember the pattern so they can gain access.

So slow down and look around you before you start entering your PIN to make sure no one is in a position where they can observe your PIN. Taking the extra time will improve your security and help protect your information and your mobile device.

Stowing your mobile device: This almost goes without saying, but you need to keep your mobile devices safe from theft. Keep them in your pocket, in a case, or in a purse/backpack and be very cautious about setting them down in public areas. Thieves are always waiting for opportunities to practice their skills and will happily relieve you of your possessions if you let down your guard.

I see a lot of people in public who seem to be tethered to their mobile devices. However, at some point you're probably going to set your mobile device down. Take a few seconds and consider your surroundings before you decide where to put your mobile device.

Do you keep it in a case on your belt? Do you put it in your purse? Do you put it in your backpack or in your back pocket? Do you leave it on the table in front of you so you can check your friends' status updates on social networking sites? Whatever your habit when it comes to putting your mobile device away, you need to consider how a thief might take advantage of your habits.

Thieves are very observant and they are successful because they look for opportunities to exploit your personal habits. The military describes the mindset as OPSEC, or Operations Security.

Try to put yourself in the role of a thief and ask yourself what you would need to do to steal your mobile device by evaluating your personal habits. It sounds kind of strange because we never think we are vulnerable until we fall victim to someone who knows how to exploit our weaknesses.

Understanding how thieves take advantage of vulnerabilities will help you know how to better protect yourself.

Tracking your mobile device: There are several ways to track your mobile device if you misplace it or someone lifts it without your knowledge. If you are constantly putting your mobile device down and then forgetting where you've put it, then you might consider an app/device combination like the hipKey(TM) by hippih ApS or the proximo(TM) by Kensington that allows you to connect a device to your keyring, belt loop, or just put it in your pocket or handbag/backpack.

The apps are downloaded to your phone (iPhone only for the hipKey(TM), or both the iPhone or Samsung GalaxyS for the Proximo(TM)) where you can configure the app to alert you with an audible alarm if you get too far away from your phone.[5][6]

There are also apps such as LoJack or Avast mobile security that will use either WiFi or GPS to help you locate and recover your stolen mobile device.[7][8] Some applications such as these will also take pictures of the person trying to unlock your mobile device after three failed PIN attempts and then email you the pictures.

LoJack's software even claims to have patented absolute persistence technology that can survive a factory reset of your device and keep on reporting your mobile devices location to allow law enforcement time to recover it.

Security Apps

I'm surprised every time I ask someone if they have anti-virus protection or other security-related apps running on their smart phone or tablet and they look at me like I've got horns growing out of my head. I personally put off getting a smart phone for a long time and only recently purchased my first smart phone in May 2014. I've always said a phone is a phone and shouldn't be used for any other purpose, but I finally succumbed to the virtual tsunami of options available and the difficulty of finding a plain old phone.

The first thing I did was research security apps and found one that met my needs. I was surprised how many options are available, especially when I ask others what they are using only to find out they aren't using any security apps. One would think there were no security apps when you find out how few people actually have them running on their mobile devices.

Bluetooth

Bluetooth is definitely a useful technology and I use it from time to time. I personally disable Bluetooth when I'm not using it because it is one feature that has been used to steal information by exploiting vulnerabilities in the technology, although the risks to newer devices is low. If you are interested in learning more about Bluetooth vulnerabilities I recommend you visit Wikipedia's page for Bluetooth and download the National Institute of Standards and Technology's "Guide to Bluetooth Security". [9],[10]

Location Services

This is also another very useful feature that I keep disabled except when I want to use it. The only risks I'm aware of are related to privacy. If your mobile device has location services enabled then any pictures you take with the mobile device are geotagged, which means location information in the form of meta-data is embedded in the pictures and allows any website capable of reading the geo-tagged information to display the location on a map such as Google Maps or Bing Maps, etc.

The location information is pretty accurate so if you don't want everyone to know where you were when you took a picture you might want to turn off location services.

Secure Email Settings/Text

Many of today's websites provide secure email by default through https. If you are using a web-based email service with your mobile device it is a good idea to ensure https is enabled. If it is a standard http connection then any email you send and receive from your mobile device over an open WiFi connection could be intercepted by anyone within range.

Your text messages are a bit different than email, so if you want a little privacy with your text messages you'll probably need to download a separate app. There are several apps that will help you encrypt your text messages.

One of the most popular apps on the Android OS is called "TextSecure" by WhisperSystems and if you want compatibility across platforms (iOS and Android) then you might try ChatSecure developed by the Guardian Project.[11] The best thing about both of these apps is they're FREE!

References

[1] David Eitelbach. Mobile Security Guide: Everything You Need to Know. *Toms Guide*.
http://www.tomsguide.com/us/mobile-security-guide,review-1918-5.html

[2] Vanja Svajcer. Sophos Mobile Security Threat Report. *SophosLabs*.
http://www.sophos.com/en-us/medialibrary/PDFs/other/sophos-mobile-security-threat-report.pdf

[3] Cisco Annual Security Report 2014. *Cisco*. http://www.cisco.com/web/offer/gist_ty2_asset/Cisco_2014_ASR.pdf

[4] Smartphone thefts rose to 3.1 million last year, Consumer Reports finds. http://www.consumerreports.org/cro/news/2014/04/smart-phone-thefts-rose-to-3-1-million-last-year/index.htm

[5] Always by Your Side. hipKey(TM). http://www.hippih.com/hipkey

[6] Proximo Find Your Phone Easy. Proximo(TM). http://www.kensington.com/us/us/4570/proximo-find-your-phone-items-easily#.U90mJJRdV14

[7] Recover Stolen Laptops, Smartphones and Tablets with Absolute LoJack. *Absolute Lojack.* http://lojack.absolute.com/en

[8] avast! Free Mobile Security. Avast. http://www.avast.com/en-us/free-mobile-security

[9] Wikipedia contributors, "Bluetooth," *Wikipedia, The Free Encyclopedia,* http://en.wikipedia.org/w/index.php?title=Bluetooth&oldid=619443262

[10] John Padgette, Karen Scarfone and Lily Chen. Guide to Bluetooth Security. National Institute of Standards and Technology http://www.nist.gov/customcf/get_pdf.cfm?pub_id=911133

[11] Molly Wood. Privacy Please: Tools to Shield your Smartphone. New York Times. http://www.nytimes.com/2014/02/20/technology/personaltech/privacy-please-tools-to-shield-your-smartphone-from-snoopers.html?_r=0

SECURITY FOCUSED SOFTWARE

Table 1. Antivirus Software - *Note: The prices shown generally reflect the cost of the antivirus product for one year unless otherwise stated.		
Ad-Aware Free Antivirus+ 10	http://www.lavasoft.com	Free
AhnLab V3 Click	http://global.ahnlab.com/en/site/main/main.do	$49.99/year
Anvi Smart Defender v1.8	http://www.anvisoft.com/product/smartde-fender.html	Free
avast Free Antivirus	http://www.avast.com/en-us/index	Free
avast Rescue Disk	http://www.avast.com/en-us/index	$10.00
AVG Antivirus Free	http://www.avg.com/us-en/free-antivi-rus-download	Free
Avira Antivirus Premium	http://www.avira.com/en/for-home-avira-an-tivirus-premium	$25.89
Avira Free Antivirus	http://www.avira.com/en/avira-free-antivirus	Free
BitDefender Internet Security 2013	http://www.bitdefender.com/solutions/inter-net-security.html	$69.95 (for 3 PCs)
Bullguard Antivirus 2013	http://www.bullguard.com/products/bull-guard-antivirus-2013.aspx	$29.95
Comodo Antivirus 2013	http://antivirus.comodo.com/	Free
Comodo Cleaning Essentials	http://www.comodo.com	Free
Daily Safety Check Home Edition	http://www.dailysafetycheck.com/Default.asp	$69.00 +
Emsisoft Emergency Kit 3.0	http://www.emsisoft.com/en/software/eek/	Free
Eset NOD32 Anti-virus 5	http://www.eset.com/us/home/products/antivirus/	$39.99
Fixmestick 2013	http://store.fixmestick.com/buy	$59.99 (for 3 PCs)

Table 1 (cont'd)

F-Secure Antivirus 2013	http://www.f-secure.com/en/web/home_us/home	$39.99 (for 3 PCs)
G Data Antivirus	http://www.gdatasoftware.com	$39.95 (for 3 PCs)
HitmanPro 3.7 (32 & 64 Bit)	http://www.surfright.nl/en	$19.95
Immunet	http://www.immunet.com	Free
Immunet Plus	http://www.immunet.com	$24.95 (1 PC)
Kaspersky Antivirus 2013	http://usa.kaspersky.com	$59.95 (for 3 PCs)
Malwarebites Anti-Malware 1.51	http://www.malwarebytes.org	$24.95
Malwarebites Anti-Malware Free 1.51	http://www.malwarebytes.org	Free
McAfee Antivirus Plus 2013	http://home.mcafee.com/store/antivirus-plus?ctst=1	$49.99
Microsoft Security Essentials	http://windows.microsoft.com/en-US/windows/security-essentials-download	Free
Norman Antivirus 10	http://safeground.norman.com	$55.00 (approx)
Norman Malware Cleaner	http://safeground.norman.com/home_and_small_office/trials_downloads/malware_cleaner	Free
Norton Antivirus 2013	http://us.norton.com/antivirus/	$49.99 (1 PC)
Outpost Antivirus Pro	http://www.agnitum.com/products/antivirus/index.php	$39.95 (3 PCs)
Panda Antivirus Pro 2013	http://www.pandasecurity.com/homeusers/solutions/antivirus/	$50.99 (3 PCs)
Panda Cloud Antivirus Free	http://www.cloudantivirus.com/en/forHome/	Free
PC Tools Spyware Doctor with AV	http://www.pctools.com/spyware-doctor/download/	$39.99 (3 PCs)
Roboscan Internet Security Free	http://www.roboscan.com/home/home_main.aspx	Free
SecureIT	http://www.secureitdirect.com/antivirus-antispyware-secureit.php	$1.95/month
Sophos Virus Removal Tool Free	http://www.sophos.com/en-us/products/free-tools/virus-removal-tool.aspx	Free
Spybot Search and Destroy	http://www.safer-networking.org/	Free

Table 1 (cont'd)

thirtyseven4 Antivirus 2013	http://www.thirtyseven4.com/	$49.95 (2 PCs)
Trendmicro Titanium Antivirus	http://www.trendmicro.com/us/home/products/titanium/index.html	$39.95 (1 PC)
TrustPort Antivirus	http://www.trustport.com/en/products/trustport-antivirus	$55.00 (3 PCs)
V3 Secure Cloud	http://www.v3securecloud.com/v3sc/pc.aspx	$29.95 (1 PC)
Viper Antivirus	http://www.vipreantivirus.com/	$39.95 (1 PC)
Webroot SecureAnwhere Complete 2013	http://www.webroot.com/En_US/consumer-products-secureanywhere-complete.html	$79.99 (5 PCs)
Zone Alarm Free	http://www.zonealarm.com/security/en-us/zonealarm-free-antivirus-firewall.htm	Free

Table 2. Online Virus Scanners	
Avast Online	http://onlinescan.avast.com/
BitDefender	http://www.bitdefender.com/scan8/index.html
Clamwin Online	http://www.clamwin.com/content/view/89/85/
Comodo Online	http://personalfirewall.comodo.com/scan/avscanner.html
ESET Online	http://www.eset.com/us/online-scanner/
F-Secure Online	http://www.f-secure.com/en/web/labs_global/removal-tools
McAfee	http://us.mcafee.com/root/mfs/default.asp?cid=13121
Panda Software	http://www.pandasoftware.com/activescan
Symantec	http://www.symantec.com/cgi-bin/securitycheck.cgi
Trendmicro	http://housecall.trendmicro.com/
Virus Total by Google	https://www.virustotal.com/

Table 3. Internet Filtering Software & Accountability (Not all offer both options)		
Accountable2you	http://www.accountable2you.com/	$4.99 per month per account
Bsecure Online	http://www.bsecure.com/	$49.95 per year (3 PCs)
Covenant Eyes	http://www.covenanteyes.com/	$17.49 per month (3 PCs)
Cyber Patrol	http://www.cyberpatrol.com/	$39.95 per year (3 PCs)
Family Fellowship	www.familyfellowship.com/	$49.95 per year (5 PCs)
Hedge Builders	http://www.hedgebuilders.com/	$5.99 per month (3 PCs)

Table 3 (cont'd)

iBoss Home	http://www.iboss.com/home_overview.html	$49.95 for iboss router plus $59.95 yearly. No per system license required.
K9 Web Protection	http://www1.k9webprotection.com/	Free
Mobicip *Designed for most mobile devices (iPhone, Android, etc) and also works with laptops.	http://www.mobicip.com/	$4.99 for basic features $9.99 annual subscription for advanced features.
NetNanny	http://www.netnanny.com/	$59.98 per year (3 PCs)
Saavi Accountability	https://www.saaviaccountability.com/	$9.00 per month (4 PCs)
WiseChoice	http://www.wisechoice.net/	$49.95 per year (3 PCs)
X3Watch	http://www.x3watch.com/	Free
X3Watch Pro	http://www.x3watch.com/	$7.00 per month (10 PCs)

Table 4. Whole Disk/Folder/File/Cloud Encryption Software		
BoxCryptor FREE	https://www.boxcryptor.com/	Free (One User)
BoxCryptor Unlimited Personal	https://www.boxcryptor.com/	$49.99 (One User)
MAC OS X FileVault	http://support.apple.com/kb/HT4790	Free with OS X 10.3 +
Microsoft BitLocker®	http://windows.microsoft.com/en-US/windows-vista/BitLocker-Drive-Encryption-Overview	Free with Windows 7 Ultimate/Enterprise, Windows 8 Professional, Windows Server 2008
Microsoft EFS	http://windows.microsoft.com/en-US/windows-vista/What-is-Encrypting-File-System-EFS	Free with Windows 2000, Windows XP Professional, Windows Server 2003
Symantec Drive Encryption	http://www.symantec.com	$110 per year

Table 5. Keystroke Encryption		
KeyScrambler Personal	http://www.qfxsoftware.com	Free
KeyScrambler Pro	http://www.qfxsoftware.com	$29.99
KeyScrambler Premium	http://www.qfxsoftware.com	$44.99
SpyShelter Free	http://www.spyshelter.com/	Free

Table 5 (cont'd)

SpyShelter Premium	http://www.spyshelter.com/	20€ or Approx $27.00
Zemana Antilogger Free	http://www.zemana.com	Free
Zemana Antilogger	http://www.zemana.com	$29.00
GuardedID	http://www.guardedid.com	$29.99 (2 PCs)
PrivacyKeyboard™	http://www.privacykeyboard.com	$57.75
Anti-Keylogger *This software is a bit dated.	http://www.anti-keyloggers.com	$28.31 (discounts for additional licenses)

Table 6. Password Management Software		
PassPack Free	https://www.passpack.com	Account required. Free unless you need the features of Pro, Group, Team, or Biz. Compatible with most modern browsers. YubiKey Compatible.
LastPass Free	https://www.lastpass.com	Account required. Free unless you want to enable two factor authentication. Compatible with most browsers. Offers support for mobile devices. Windows, MAC, Linux YubiKey Compatible.
Password Tote	https://www.passwordtote.com	Account required. Free for a basic account with ads. $7.99 a year for a Browser account and $2.99 a month for a software account. YubiKey Compatible.
Keepass	https://www.keepass.info	Software based. Does not require an account. Free. Windows only. YubiKey Compatible.
Keygenius	http://kg.yubico.com/	Account required. Compatible with most browsers. Requires Greasemonkey plugin. Free with a YubiKey.
Password Safe	http://passwordsafe.sourceforge.net/	Software based. Does not require an account. Free. Windows only. YubiKey Compatible.

Table 6 (cont'd)

SuperGenPass	http://supergenpass.com/	Free. No software or accounts required. Compatible with most browsers. Windows, MAC, Linux, Mobile
RoboForm	http://www.roboform.com	Free to try. $9.95 - $39.95 depending on the version. Windows, MAC, Linux, Mobile
Kaspersky Password Manager	http://usa.kaspersky.com	$24.95 Windows, MAC, Linux
Iron Key Personal	http://www.ironkey.com	$89.00 - $599.00 Windows, MAC, Linux
Passter	http://www.passter.com	

Table 7. Anti-Theft/Laptop Recovery Software		
LoJack for Laptops Standard Edition	http://www3.absolute.com/lojackforlaptops/	$39.99 Windows, MAC
LoJack for Laptops Premium Edition	http://www3.absolute.com/lojackforlaptops/	$59.99 Windows, MAC
Laptop Cop	http://www.laptopcopsoftware.com	$49.95 Windows
Gadget Track	http://www.gadgettrak.com/	$19.95 Windows, MAC
Undercover	http://www.orbicule.com/undercover/mac/	$49.00 MAC
FrontDoorSoftware Basic	http://www.frontdoorsoftware.com/	FREE Windows, MAC
FrontDoorSoftware Deluxe	http://www.frontdoorsoftware.com/	$29.95 (1 PC for 3 years) Windows, MAC
Prey	http://preyproject.com/	FREE (Open Source) Windows, MAC, Linux, Android, iOS
Prey Pro	http://preyproject.com/	$5.00 per month Windows, MAC, Linux, Android, iOS

Table 8. Firewall Software (You need a spare computer with 2 NICs)
For home or SOHO networks.
****Don't let the "FREE" fool you. These are very good products and fairly uncomplicated to setup if you have a little time and patience.

Untangle	http://www.untangle.com/	FREE
Sophos	https://www.sophos.com/en-us.aspx	FREE
pfSense	https://www.pfsense.org/	FREE
GUFW	http://gufw.org/	FREE

Appendix Two

Self Help Videos & Tutorials

Self Help Videos

When I first started working on this book I thought I would put together a lot of tutorials. After I became more familiar with what was available I decided the most important thing I could focus on were the key principals that you can implement to make your online experience a little more secure. This section contains links to some very useful videos you can use to give you step by step help to implement some of the principals I discussed in each chapter. This list of videos with links follows the outline of my book and I hoped they would be helpful when you are applying the principals you feel best meet your needs.

Note: All the links in this section have been shortened using the Google url shortner or the YouTube url shortner as appropriate.

Modems & Routers

Video Title	HTML Link
James Lyne: Everyday cybercrime — and what you can do about it	http://goo.gl/uFA2Tn
Linksys Router: Change the Default Admin Password (Tutorial)	http://goo.gl/zGmJiz
Netgear Router: Change the Default Admin Password (Tutorial)	http://goo.gl/fdyaus
Apple Airport: Change the Default Admin Password (Tutorial)	http://goo.gl/nMrufS
Linksys Wireless Network: Set a WPA Password (Tutorial)	http://goo.gl/rmxpHW
Netgear Wireless Network: Set a WPA Password (Tutorial)	http://goo.gl/yPQYPx
Apple Airport Wireless Network: Set a WPA Password (Tutorial)	http://goo.gl/WTWyQe

Video Title	HTML Link
Linksys Wireless Network: Restrict Access by MAC Address (Tutorial)	http://goo.gl/HNPKXY
Netgear Wireless Network: Restrict Access by MAC Address (Tutorial)	http://goo.gl/ty8Gcr
Apple Airport Wireless Network: Restrict Access by MAC Address (Tutorial)	http://goo.gl/wY8YtO
Protect your computer with Windows Vista Firewall	http://youtu.be/vq-vjJsU7no
Windows 7 Firewall Tutorial	http://youtu.be/uocnTrnP8Bs
Windows Firewall Complete Guide for Windows 8	http://youtu.be/Xqvn1jOsW70
Start the Built-in Firewall in Mac OS X (Tutorial)	http://goo.gl/HDT3iy
Linksys Tutorial Videos for Smart Wi-Fi Setup	http://goo.gl/Pknkdu
D-Link Routers: How to configure DHCP reservation	http://youtu.be/HooBrKjRkeA
D-Link Routers: How to configure parental controls on your router	http://youtu.be/itCdzXPkrU4
D-Link Routers: How to connect wireless with MAC OS.	http://youtu.be/Domhud98lD4
D-Link Routers: How to connect wireless in Windows 8	http://youtu.be/akP3gySEabE
D-Link Routers: How to factory reset your router	http://youtu.be/J6MIY-EhL3E
D-Link Routers: How to configure the wireless settings on your router	http://youtu.be/tAobMGgJPdQ
D-Link Routers: How to log into your router	http://youtu.be/1Qu8kEPiXmg
D-Link Routers: How to connect wireless in Windows 7	http://youtu.be/Mt_E2uEfd94
D-Link Routers: How to change or recover your wireless password	http://youtu.be/e--HxUZorzk
D-Link Routers: How to setup your router with Cable Internet	http://youtu.be/w4eeNA2GnbM
D-Link Routers: How to setup or change your router password	http://youtu.be/djhQqV-vp4Y
D-Link Routers: How to setup your router with a DSL Internet Connection	http://youtu.be/1z2VYTbH1ro
D-Link Routers: How to install the mydlink lite app on the iPhone	http://youtu.be/qm44CEalw5E
D-Link Routers: How to connect wireless using an iPhone	http://youtu.be/p6PcgWUnz1o
D-Link Routers: How to change your router's IP	http://youtu.be/4tgB199MOTc
How To: Find out if someone is stealing your Wi-Fi	http://youtu.be/MWQ9X-FU2_EY
D-link Advanced Wireless Security using a MAC Filter	http://youtu.be/SMf-2LjikPA
Linksys Advanced Wireless Security using a MAC filter	http://youtu.be/WvO6Tr2htTc
Netgear Advanced Wireless Security using a MAC filter	http://youtu.be/Loyp-EQDoLk
Fast D-Link Wireless Router Security Setup	http://youtu.be/5KfSS1mi-YM
Setting up your computer with OpenDNS	http://youtu.be/U4N0Em_Pz-g
Forcing Users to Use OpenDNS Servers Block Port 53	http://youtu.be/gsfWjR9xQpk
Configuring Your Network to Use Google Public DNS	http://youtu.be/LQJ2JL9nUqY
Mac Class - Adding/Using A Custom DNS Server (i.e. OpenDNS or Google Public DNS)	http://youtu.be/ZktuKcP1_tM

Options for Safe Search	
Internet Safety Tip #1- Locking Google SafeSearch	http://youtu.be/DC6v_wt3N94
How to Lock Google SafeSearch on your Computer. Safe Search Google for Kids!	http://youtu.be/TyYviqb37ss

Firewalls

You will also need to know how to burn an "ISO" file in order to use some of the free firewalls highlighted below. An ISO file is an image file of a CD and/or DVD that can be burned to a blank CD+/-R or DVD+/-R and allow you to install the image on a computer. This is a little more technical than some of my recommendations but is still something most people can do with a little time and patience. The videos below will guide you through the steps necessary to set up a few of the Linux firewalls as mentioned in last part of chapter three. These are designed to be setup and installed on a separate computer you can use as your dedicated firewall that will givie you outstanding protection.

Video Title	HTML Link
How to Burn an ISO to DVD	http://youtu.be/bkbQAiSEegQ
pfSense	
pfSense: How to Turn an Old PC into an Epic Router	http://youtu.be/Q0JFfpG4BWI
pfSense HOW-TO video series | HOW TO INSTALL PF-SENSE	http://youtu.be/hrgUsCgiU_M
pfSense HOW-TO video series | CONFIGURE PFSENSE via WEB GUI	http://youtu.be/97OE2BwMTsA
pfSense HOW-TO video series | HOW TO FILTER WEB BROWSING	http://youtu.be/ybzQk-VZeac
Sophos UTM Home Edition	
Setting up Sophos UTM - Training Episode 1	http://youtu.be/mx6l1f6Bpy0
Using Sophos UTM Web Protection - Training Episode 2	http://youtu.be/uI8NbEfxEs4
Using Sophos UTM Email Protection - Training Episode 3	http://youtu.be/tozOXf-L-RY
Using Sophos UTM Intrusion Protection - Training Episode 4	http://youtu.be/HDgJHFIp3Nk
How to setup Secure Sockets Layer (SSL) for a virtual private network (VPN) - Training Episode 5	http://youtu.be/GGt26ZlerpQ
Setting up Web Filtering Profiles - Training Episode 6	http://youtu.be/2v4_3bph6GA
Setting up Backup & Restore - Training Episode 7	http://youtu.be/-ShStT59GLs

Untangle Gateway	
Untangle Gateway 10.0 install and overview | How to install a free network gateway	http://youtu.be/ZkI0QbLJt2M
Install Untangle	http://youtu.be/V74Sawv1zh4

Physical Security

Video Title	HTML Link
Secure Erase / Format With bootable CD/USB Linux Parted Magic by Britec	http://youtu.be/g8t2ZXOMGKY
Hard Drive Tools : DBAN (Darik's Boot and Nuke)	http://youtu.be/iGQ-AIm8QsQ
How to Wipe Your Hard Drive: a Geek Squad 2 Minute Miracle	http://youtu.be/ewisIDG-K-E
How to destroy a hard drive part. 1 - Bang Goes The Theory - Series 6 - BBC	http://youtu.be/4WIMSP_IMGs
How to destroy a hard drive! - Part 2 - Bang Goes The Theory - Series 6 - BBC	http://youtu.be/RDZyQ4WEb7Y

Operating System Security

Video Title	HTML Link
How To Reset Mac OS X Forgotten Password	http://youtu.be/ohvlp3fPp1s
How To Protect Your Investment - Mac Hard Drive Lock-Down	http://youtu.be/Uz2LjuR_Rhs
HOWTO: Create a Limited User Account in Windows 7	http://youtu.be/H12lwqmZXmA
Windows 8 - Add/Delete/Modify User Accounts [Tutorial]	http://youtu.be/7N42jqzHyCE
How to use Windows 8.1 WITHOUT a Microsoft Account	http://youtu.be/HwEFU0cIEUQ
Mac OS X User Accounts and Security	http://youtu.be/GdIBH31T5C0
Mac OS X - How to Disable : Enable Guest Account	http://youtu.be/V3OM7xFvu7c
How To Use BitLocker To Go In Windows 8	http://youtu.be/voWj542eEKQ
Bit Locker Drive Encryption in Microsoft Windows Vista	http://youtu.be/7qyE02WvCTo
Encryption on Mac OSX Mountain Lion	http://youtu.be/udvfenYkIRU
ABC News Report - New Online Scam by Keyloggers	http://youtu.be/P1WLbqGbLl8
How to Secure Your Computer	http://youtu.be/-goxn384ewA
SkyCrypt - Cloud Encryption for Any Cloud Service Provider www.SkyCrypt.com	http://youtu.be/ihf0RzKAcfc
Encrypting Your Word Document for Google Drive : Microsoft Office Tips	http://youtu.be/dSYqTwZWCrw
How to encrypt a document in Microsoft Word 2010	http://youtu.be/jqpb3-SM-io

27- Libre Office - Calc, Open Office -- Calc, Excel Tutorial -- Password Protect and Read Only	http://youtu.be/LbJKQWP1p-o
How To Password Protect Files, Folders, Documents	http://youtu.be/kVCXv0rl3dU

Passwords

Video Title	HTML Link
6 "Digital Life" Hacks, for Your Passwords!	http://youtu.be/hYyWgPXfx9U
How to choose a strong password - simple tips for better security	http://youtu.be/VYzguTdOmmU
How to Choose Strong Passwords	http://youtu.be/COU5T-Wafa4
Creating a Secure Password	http://youtu.be/fFMGaUH6qh0
How To Create Strong Secure Passwords	http://youtu.be/cUH3tQbGj4A
Protect Your Accounts Through Strong Passwords	http://youtu.be/mlVl2OPhIVk
Lastpass screencast training tutorial	http://youtu.be/ejit3hRyjDE
Dashlane - Setting Up Your Dashlane Account	http://youtu.be/o7ExX3Q0y6s
1Password	http://youtu.be/Smv_SvEpYZI
KeePass Tutorial	http://youtu.be/YiiFT1JLQTs
What is Multifactor Authentication?	http://youtu.be/XgSeCjcVBAA

Browser Security

Video Title	HTML Link
Cyber Security: How To Protect Yourself Online	http://youtu.be/qjxkceLBFtA
Cyber Security Part 2: It Never Leaves the Internet	http://youtu.be/R-fxxVwzHP0
Cyber Security Part 3: Secure Your Online Applications	http://youtu.be/RyO9u-eLtpM
Cyber Security 4: Windows, Email, and Browser Security	http://youtu.be/LtrC_HdfaOc
Protect Yourself From Phishing Attacks	http://youtu.be/kjafzaRiBTI
Protect Yourself From Online Shopping Scams	http://youtu.be/sEF1tR9rsYg
Protect Yourself From Cyber-Spying Criminals	http://youtu.be/fuUWPNreZuo
Warning! Fake Job Offers Lead To ID Theft	http://youtu.be/JuDHHIlRi6s
How to Stay Secure Through Updates & Patches	http://youtu.be/LsNI63f-K0E
Protect Your Facebook Login Credentials	http://youtu.be/fuiuQzyXmYQ
Disable Java web plugin in Apple® Safari on Mac® OS X™	http://youtu.be/W4BCNwq3Vzo
Java 7 Security Flaw + How to Disable Java 7	http://youtu.be/QFHShFKbLxk
Enable/Disable JavaScript in Internet Explorer Windows 8	http://youtu.be/jwysSRTcxj0
How to use tracking protection lists and ActiveX filtering	http://youtu.be/xijzxBPAY4U
How to Turn ON ActiveX Filtering in Internet Explorer® 11 on Windows® 8.1 PC	http://youtu.be/R2YHTXezNEg
Sandboxie Review 2013	http://youtu.be/XnVZ4uAz55I
Symantec Guide to Scary Internet Stuff - No 4 Drive-by downloads	http://youtu.be/J0QXD2ts4Qc
Symantec Guide to Scary Internet Stuff - Botnets	http://youtu.be/SubxMZxhiKo
Symantec Guide to Scary Internet Stuff - No 5 Misleading Applications	http://youtu.be/GaA6UV9iQOo
Protect Yourself Online	http://youtu.be/9eEdFqxqmDk

Email

Video Title	HTML Link
AVOIDING SPAM	http://youtu.be/7syinn7VMrM
Avoiding phishing, spam, and scams	http://youtu.be/AoNFv1mRrrA
How to avoid phishing e-mail scams - Which? Consumer Rights	http://youtu.be/WwFX-3RISbU
Symantec Guide to Scary Internet Stuff - Phishing	http://youtu.be/K8lWLwuiDwk
GnuPG Tutorial Part 1: Installation	http://youtu.be/HuLr8PdkdOY
GnuPG Tutorial Part 2: Generating Keys	http://youtu.be/0WOVMheeepk
GnuPG Tutorial Part 3: Exchanging Keys	http://youtu.be/dIW_mDD8EPc
GnuPG Tutorial Part 4: Importing Keys	http://youtu.be/moeMgmGPoMY
GnuPG Tutorial Part 5: Encrypting	http://youtu.be/lQs0Zs2rURA

Mobile Device Security

Video Title	HTML Link
Simple Tips For Secure Mobile Banking	http://youtu.be/pSUqC0tdsz4
The Risks and Rewards of Mobile Apps - Symantec	http://youtu.be/MzT_hm1_ohw
Cybercrime Goes Mobile - Trend Micro	http://youtu.be/D5DIOZzwsEc
Mod06 Mobile Device Security Awareness Video	http://youtu.be/8xQ7-qbjGzE
Brian Tokuyoshi Talks About Mobile Security at Infosecurity 2014	http://youtu.be/fW8j4erBWzI
IT Security Best Practices - What Are Some Mobile Security Risks?	http://youtu.be/G44wgLOLXTk
Mobile Device Security Best Practices - CompTIA A+ 220-802: 3.3	http://youtu.be/U45JK6hXkvU
Device Advice | Smartphone Security Tips | Verizon Wireless	http://youtu.be/_NQiXTk6QPw
Smartphone Security	http://youtu.be/Xz9PVLOa0hI

SAMPLE NETWORK DOCUMENTATION

Internet Service Provider

Provider	Service Type	Support Number	Account Number	PPPoE	User Name	Password
Comcast	Cable	1-800-555-5555	123456			

Computing Hardware

Computers/Devices	Make	Model	IP Address	MAC Address
Jack's Computer	HP	Pavillion D9000	10.0.0.3	FD:13:27:E1:F8:AC
Jill's Laptop	Dell	Inspiron 3500	10.0.0.4	FD:13:27:E1:F8:AE
Sue's iPad	Apple	iPad Gen 4	10.0.0.5	FD:13:27:E1:F8:A1
Billy's Android Phone	Samsung	S4	10.0.0.5	FD:13:27:E1:F8:AF
Printer	Brother	HL-2240		

Networking Devices

Modem/Routers/Switches	Make	Model	IP Address	MAC Address	User Name/Password
Cable Modem	ARRIS	Surfboard SB6141	192.168.100.1	FD:13:27:E1:F8:EE	No User ID/yourPassword
WiFi Router	NetGear	WNDR3400	10.0.0.1	EE:14.22:AE:F3:E1	Admin/yourPassword

Router Security

DHCP Range	Security Options	SSID	Wireless Key/Pass Phrase	DNS Servers
10.0.0.3 – 10.0.0.10	WPA2-PSK [AES]	Your SSID	4DB678AEFG32DEIL89K	199.85.126.20 & 199.85.127.20

Email Information

POP Server	SMTP Server	IMAP Server	Web Address	User Name/Password
Your POP Server	Your SMTP Server	Your IMAP Server	Your Webmail Address	Your User Name/Your Password

129

Index

ABOUT THE AUTHOR

Terence Sadler is a security professional with more than 30 years experience and education in information technology, cybersecurity, information assurance/information systems security, risk management, operations security, training development, and security program management.

He served as a Cryptologic Technician in the United States Navy which fueled his interest in security. During an assignment in West Virginia, he served as the Operations Security Officer and he also became certified as a National Cryptologic School (NCS) facilitator for OPSEC fundamentals. Operations Security, better known as OPSEC in the military, is a formalized risk management process which enables one to consider an operation or activity from the perspective of an adversary in order to identify critical information and apply measures to protect it from unintentional disclosure. During his last tour, he served as the Information Systems Security Manager (ISSM)/Network Operations Center Chief where he really began to understand how important it is for everyone to learn about cybersecurity.

His military awards include two Navy and Marine Corps Commendation medals and six Navy and Marine Corps Achievement medals.

Following his career in the Navy, he became a security specialist for the United States Army where he qualified as a Certified Information System Security Professional (CISSP)*. He has a Bachelor of Arts in Communications Studies from the University of Maryland, University College and a Master of Science Information Assurance: Cyber Security with Graduate Honors through Regis University.

---

* CISSP is a registered mark of the International Information Systems Security Certification Consortium in the United States and other countries.

We hope you found *Cybersecurity for Everyone* helpful and useful for your home and/or business.

For access to additional materials and resources, please visit the Compass North Group website at:
www.cybersecurityforeveryone.com

We also invite you to visit the Signalman Publishing online catalog at www.signalmanpublishing.com for other useful and thought-provoking titles.

Bulk orders are available for discount direct from the publisher. Please contact via email: info@signalmanpublishing.com.

SIGNALMAN
PUBLISHING

CPSIA information can be obtained
at www.ICGtesting.com
Printed in the USA
LVOW04s1551020616

490960LV00016B/769/P